Religion and Citizenship

GCSE Religious Studies for **AQA B**

Lesley Parry,
Jan Hayes and Kim Hands

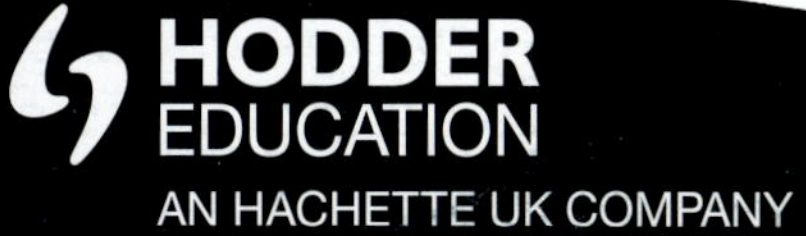

Acknowledgements
Thanks should go to David who wrote the AQA course. Writing a book for the course has been an interesting journey!

Citizenship is all about respect and harmony – communities made up of all kinds of folk getting along and supporting each other. The writing team certainly did this to produce this book. Hopefully this book will help to generate a bit more respect and harmony.

We dedicate this book to the memory of Warren David Parry (1967–2008).

The Publishers would like to thank the following for permission to reproduce copyright material:
Photo credits
Cover © Steve Cole/Anyone/amanaimages/Corbis **p.5** *tc* © David Hancock/Alamy, *tl & tr* © Photodisc/Getty Images, *cl* © Royalty Free/Corbis, *cr* © Andres Rodrigues/Alamy, *b* © Rob Wilkinson/Alamy; **p.11** *both* © Lesley Parry; **p. 12** *t* © Carlos Davila/Alamy, *b* © Lesley Parry; **p.14** *l* © Buccina Studios/Photodisc/Getty Images, *r* © World Religions Photo Library/Alamy; **p.15** © Peter Dazeley/photographer's Choice/ Getty Images; **p.19** *all* © Lesley Parry; **p.22** *l* © SGP/Rex Features, *r* © Sipa Press/Rex Features; **p. 23** © Lesley Parry; **p.24** *c* © Clive Brunskill/ Getty Images, *tr* © Matthew Ashton/PA Photos, *cr* © Bob Thomas/Corbis, *br* © Bob Thomas/Getty Images; **p.25** *t* © nvicta Kent Media/Rex Features, *b* © Lesley Parry; **p.26** Reproduced with kind permission of Christians in Sport; **p.27** *t* © Topical Press Agency/Hulton Archive/Getty Images, *b* © Stu Forster/Getty Images; **p.28** *l* © North Wind Picture Archives/Alamy, *cl* © P Hillyard/Newspix/Rex Features, *c* © KPA/Zuma/Rex Features, *cr* © Lakruwan Wanniarachchi/AFP/Getty Images, *r* © Offside/Rex Features; **p.29** *l* © Sipa Press/Rex Features, *r* © Travis Lindquist/Getty Images; **p.30** *t* Reproduced with kind permission of Kick It Out, *b* © Dennis Stone/Rex Features; **p.32** *t* & **96** *r* © Jeff Blackier/Rex Features; **p.32** *b* & **96** *l* © Rosemary Roberts/Alamy; **p.33** Reproduced with kind permission of Trades Union Congress; **p.38** *all* © Lesley Parry; **p.39**© Terry Fincher. Photo Int/Alamy; **p.41** *t* Reproduced with kind permission of The Salvation Army, *c* © The Salvation Army, *b* © Ascension Trust; **p.43** © Oli Scarff/ Getty Images; **p.45** © Lesley Parry; **p.47** *t* © The Travel Library/Rex Features, b © 2009 Singapore Post Limited; **p.48** © Susannah Ireland/ Rex Features; **p.50** © Anwar Hussein/Getty Images; **p.51** & **97** © Lesley Parry; **p.53** © Howard Davies/CORBIS; **p.57** *all* © Lesley Parry; **p.58** *tl* © Manjunath Kiran/epa/Corbis, *bl* © NARINDER NANU/AFP/Getty Images, *br* © Elkie/Alamy; **p.59** *l* © Israel images/Alamy, *r* © Roberto Herrett/Alamy; **p.62**© Lesley Parry; **p.63** © Ilene MacDonald/Alamy; **p.64** © Sipa Press/Rex Features; **p.80** *l* © Citizens Advice, *r* Copyright © NSPCC – All rights reserved. National Society for the Prevention of Cruelty to Children. ChildLine is a service provided by NSPCC, Weston House, 42 Curtain Road, London EC2A 3NH. In Scotland the ChildLine service is provided by Children 1st on behalf of the NSPCC. Registered charity numbers 216401 and SC037717; **p.81** *l* © Samaritans, *r* © picturesbyrob/Alamy; **p.83** *t* © Everett Collection/Rex Features, *b* & **99** © Alex Wong/Getty Images; **p.94** *l* © JUPITERIMAGES/Creatas/Alamy, *c* © Photodisc/Getty Images; *r* © Image Source/Rex Features.

Written sources
Scripture taken from the HOLY BIBLE, NEW INTERNATIONAL VERSION®.
Copyright © 1973, 1978, 1984 International Bible Society. Used by permission of Zondervan.
All rights reserved.
The 'NIV' and 'New International Version' trademarks are registered in the United States Patent and Trademark Office by International Bible Society. Use of either trademark requires the permission of International Bible Society.

Orders: please contact Bookpoint Ltd, 130 Milton Park, Abingdon, Oxon OX14 4SB. Telephone: +44 (0)1235 827720. Fax: +44 (0)1235 400454. Lines are open 9.00–5.00, Monday to Saturday, with a 24-hour message answering service. Visit our website at www.hoddereducation.co.uk.

First published in 2009 by
Hodder Education,
Part of Hachette UK
338 Euston Road
London NW1 3BH

Impression number 5 4 3 2 1
Year 2013 2012 2011 2010 2009

Illustrations by Oxford Illustrators and Richard Duszczak
Typeset in 11 point Minion by DC Graphic Design Limited, Swanley, Kent
Printed in Italy

A catalogue record for this title is available from the British Library.

ISBN 978 0340 98363 8

Contents

Introduction

This book has been written specifically to meet the AQA Specification B Unit 1 syllabus. It follows the unit outline, moving through the topics in the order of the unit as set out in the specification. It is informed additionally by the specification from which it grew (also called Specification B).

The unit is examined through one exam paper of 1 hour and 30 minutes. All six topics within the unit will be represented on that paper, though candidates will be required to answer questions on only four topics. Each question being worth 18 marks, and with quality of written response now within the mark scheme itself (rather than an additional sum), the total for the paper will be 72 marks. An example of the exam paper and what it should look like is found in Appendix II at the back of this book. This is annotated to help demystify the exam language and paper style.

Unit 1, when studied in conjunction with a second unit, leads to a full GCSE qualification. It could also be studied alongside a GCSE (Short) Course in Citizenship – the two courses would support each other, and very clearly develop student knowledge and understanding.

The topics within the book cover the unit content from a variety of angles, as well as providing the necessary information required by those studying for the exam. Each topic asks students to think about what they are being told, and about the implications of the issues. There are many opportunities for evaluation work, which now forms 50 per cent of the total mark for the exam. Knowledge and understanding of the topics are important, but ability to apply that knowledge is vital to achieve the highest grades. The style of text is designed to encourage and develop exactly that.

Exam technique is a constant theme, as it can cost candidates many marks if poor. It is worth using class time to teach/learn good techniques via the mechanics of good answers. The authors of this book are all senior examiners with AQA, and have lengthy experience in their roles. This book gives good advice, so make good use of it!

The specification allows centres to prepare candidates to answer from one or more religious traditions on any question. This book allows study of a single religious tradition, or of several – all religious traditions are commented on for each element within each topic.

Given this is an issues course, students should be encouraged to collect their own examples of the issues as met in the news. They can collect, add comments, give their own opinion and even try to say what they think religion(s) would say. This will help with their recall and provide real examples to call on in the exam. The specification speaks of local issues and responses to them – be sure to give examples of these, and make sure your classes know about local organisations and their work in response to any of the topics in this course.

A revision outline in Appendix I is designed to support revision, but can act as a checklist for students as they move through the course.

About this course

This course gets you to think about six key issues linked to Citizenship. Some of these will have affected you directly, or you will have direct experience of them. Some you will know of through other people's experience. Some you may only know of through the media. Keep in mind that you already have a whole load of knowledge about these issues, and you can use this in your exam.

For the exam, you have to answer questions on four of the topics. All six topics will always be on the exam paper – you just answer questions on four of them. Actually, you could answer more, because they'll still get marked, and the four best-answered questions get taken forward as your marks. HOWEVER, people who do this often don't get great marks. It is only a good idea to do this if you have finished answering your chosen four questions – at *your* right speed (not having rushed) – and still have loads of time left.

As you read through the issues, you will have opinions and attitudes to them. This is good! You will be asked about your own opinion to many of the issues as part of the exam. Therefore, do take the chances to discuss and explain your own opinions – it helps you to present them better in the exam when you have to.

Keep your eye on the news – there will be lots of stories that link to these issues in the time it takes to do this course. These stories could figure in exam papers, which are written about fifteen months before you get to sit the exam, and often use topical stories. They certainly give you a bigger range of examples to use in your answers when you are trying to explain or back-up a point. Could it be time to start a scrapbook?!

The religious bit

Religion also has opinions on these issues. This is an RE course, after all, so you are going to see the attitudes of some religions. You will have to write about them in the exam if you want to get good grades. This means trying to understand what those attitudes are and where they come from – in other words, the beliefs and teachings of the religions. In this book, you'll be given a small number of beliefs and teachings for each religion on each topic. Quite often you can use these teachings in a few different topics (which always helps!). If a teaching will apply to more than one topic, use it.

This double page gives you some general teachings that you can apply to all the different topics. It cuts down the number of teachings you have to learn and means you understand these quite strongly. However, the best answers in exams always use beliefs and teachings that are specific to the topics, as well as the general ones. Don't forget to learn some of these when you meet them later. Bookmark this page, or copy the teachings into the front of your book or file. Then use them as the basis for your work. When you study a topic, refer back to these teachings to help you work out what the religious attitude will be to that topic.

Buddhism 

1 Reincarnation and karma – our words, thoughts and deeds create energies that shape our future rebirths. We need to make sure these are positive.
2 The Five Precepts (guidelines for living) – not harming others (ahimsa); using language kindly; not taking what is not freely given; not clouding our minds; no sexual misconduct.
3 Compassion (loving kindness).

Christianity ✝

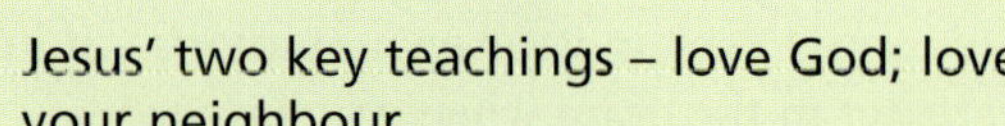

1 Jesus' two key teachings – love God; love your neighbour.
2 Equality of all because, in Genesis, we are told that God made each of us.
3 Justice (fairness) – since everyone is equal, everyone deserves fairness.
4 Forgiveness and love are ideas taught by Jesus and shown in his actions.

Hinduism ॐ

Hindu holy books list many virtues:

1 Ahimsa (non-violence).
2 Self-discipline.
3 Tolerance.
4 Service to others.
5 Compassion.
6 Providing shelter/support to others.
7 Respect for all life.
8 Wisdom.
9 Honesty with others and oneself.
10 Cleanliness.

Islam ☪

1 The ummah – brotherhood of all Muslims. This means that all Muslims are equal and deserve equal respect and treatment.
2 Everyone has to follow duties set by Allah, for example, the Five Pillars.
3 Shari'ah law – Muslim law stemming from the Qur'an and Hadith and applied to modern life by Islamic scholars.

Judaism

The Ten Commandments are found in the book of Genesis in the Torah:

1 Love only G-d.
2 Make no idols of G-d.
3 Do not take G-d's name in vain.
4 Keep the Shabbat holy.
5 Respect your parents.
6 Do not kill.
7 Do not steal.
8 Do not commit adultery.
9 Do not tell lies.
10 Do not be jealous of what others have.

Sikhism

The Khalsa vows:

1 Meditation and service to the one God, including worship, following the teachings and wearing the Five Ks as a mark of the faith and devotion to it.
2 Do not use intoxicants.
3 Do not eat meat that has been ritually slaughtered (most Sikhs are vegetarians).
4 The equality of all people, leading to respect for all and a desire to fight injustice, and including not hurting others by theft or deed.
5 Sikh ethical virtues – sharing with others, including tithing (sewa); dutifulness; prudence; justice; tolerance; temperance; chastity; patience; contentment; detachment and humility.

Task

Below are some of the issues covered in this course. Choose a religion and read the teachings. How do you think your chosen religion would react to the following situations? Would they consider them right or wrong or neither?

a Someone having an affair.
b A person not being allowed to join a sports team because of their disability.
c A factory owner paying the lowest wages possible to increase profit.
d A minority ethnic group being harassed.
e A religious believer being 'out and proud' about their religion.
f Young people protesting violently for animal rights.

What you just did was to show that you can make good guesses about religious attitudes using limited information. Well done.

Topic One Religion and relationships

This topic is about the relationships we have, especially personal and sexual relationships. It considers how those relationships are formed and expressed in our society. A big part of the topic is concerned with **marriage** and **family** life. We also have to be able to evaluate what society allows and encourages in relation to what religions say.

Generally speaking, religions expect everyone who is not married to live a life of **celibacy** and **chastity**. In our society though, it is more and more common for people to not marry but still have sexual relationships.

Let's talk sex!

Why do people have sex? Love, lust, fun, money, to make life – any more ideas?

Is it always okay to have sex? When do you think sex isn't okay – under what circumstances?

It is true to say that society changes all the time. Fifty years ago, it was illegal to be gay and there was widespread persecution of homosexuals. Today, it isn't such a big deal and most young people don't see it as an issue (whether they themselves are gay or not). Fifty years ago, almost everyone got married and **divorce** was rare. Today, fewer than half of us marry, and half of those that do then get divorced! As society changes our attitudes to sex change. However, religions have kept a consistent attitude over time, because it is based on beliefs and teachings. For this course, you need to be aware of both secular (what society says/does) and religious attitudes.

Look at these comments. What is your opinion of each?

My Dad had an affair. He and my mum stayed together though.

Kit

My mate told me he's gay. He's the captain of the rugby team!

Sal

My boyfriend and I intend to move in together when we finish school and get jobs.

Elsa

I will stay pure and not have sex before I marry.

Isa

Key terms

Adultery to have an affair (sex with someone other than your husband or wife).

Age of consent the age at which a person is considered old enough to be able to decide to have sex, according to the law.

Celibacy not having sexual relations.

Chastity keeping oneself sexually pure, e.g. waiting until marriage before having sex.

Commitment the act of making a promise or pledge.

Contraception precautions taken to prevent pregnancy and to protect against sexually transmitted infections.

Contract a binding, formal agreement between two sides.

Covenant an agreement based on promises between two sides; often linked to religion, so includes an agreement before and with God.

Heterosexuality being physically attracted to the opposite sex.

Homosexuality being physically attracted to the same sex.

Responsibility a duty; a legal or moral obligation; something we have to do.

Now you know the key terms for this topic

Sexuality

Celibacy

I am celibate. I have no sexual partner. I have made a decision to wait until I marry to have sex. If I never marry, then I'll not have sex.

Heterosexuality

We met at school and just fell for each other. We broke up a few times, and then drifted apart. But we got back together at a school reunion four years ago, and knew we needed to make it work this time. Our relationship is really strong.

Homosexuality

We met at university and have been together ever since. We are having a ***civil partnership*** *this year. This is a strong, loving, sexual relationship – and it works for us.*

Age of consent

This is when you are old enough by ***law*** *to choose to have sex. It is 16 years old. Of course, you could have sex before then – but you aren't considered mature enough to be responsible, and it is against the law.*

Sex before marriage

We all had sexual relationships before being married to anyone. There were different circumstances and reasons for this. Perhaps because we were part of a relationship, perhaps because it was lust – you know, one-night stands – and fun, perhaps because we were in a relationship leading to marriage, or perhaps just because everyone else was doing it.

Adultery

Even though we are married, I had an affair. It lasted a few months. It has taken a long time to begin to make up for it. The marriage really took a battering, and is still fragile, but we are working on it.

Task

1. Evaluative (AO2) questions make up half of the total mark. With a partner, work out as many reasons to agree and disagree with each of these statements:
   a. **There shouldn't be an age of consent.**
   b. **Only married couples should have sex.**

Please note: models used for illustrative purposes only.

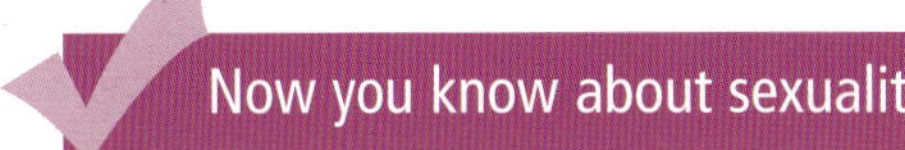

Contraception

The exam could ask you about attitudes to **contraception** and why (religious) people prefer one kind over another. Let's think about these issues.

Why use contraception?

Read these statements and decide why these people use contraception.

I'm not ready to be a dad, but I do have sex. – **Ben**

I'm HIV positive and I don't want to pass that on to my partner. We still enjoy sex. – **Sarah**

Well, I like the fun of using contraceptives when I am having sex. It's all part of the enjoyment for me. – **Shane**

So what types of contraception are there?

There are many types available, and they work in different ways. This is why some people use one kind, but not another. Religious people especially will accept the use of some methods of contraception, but not others.

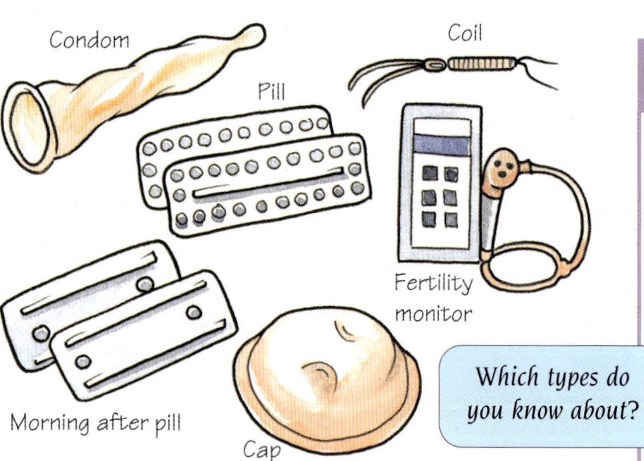

Which types do you know about?

- Artificial methods – contraceptive devices that are made and then used, like a condom.
- Natural methods – contraceptive practices or behaviours aimed at limiting the chance of pregnancy, such as the rhythm method.
- Permanent methods – operations to prevent either the production of an egg or sperm permanently. These are the only ones that are 100 per cent guaranteed to prevent pregnancy.

Try to work out which type of contraceptive is being described in each of the following statements.

1. The withdrawal method (where a man withdraws from inside the woman before he ejaculates) is a commonly used, but very unreliable, attempt to avoid pregnancy.
2. Barrier contraceptives make a barrier between the egg and sperm. If they don't meet, there is no pregnancy.
3. A man can have an operation, as can a woman, called sterilisation. This stops either sperm or eggs being released, so pregnancy can't happen.
4. During the month, there are times when a woman is more fertile than at other times. By working out her cycles a couple can try to avoid pregnancy.
5. Using a coil (IUD) makes the woman menstruate even if there is a fertilised egg in her womb. Therefore, the egg is lost with the blood.
6. The Pill affects a woman's hormones putting certain chemicals into her system. This stops egg production.

Task

1. Imagine you're a doctor. Recommend a form of contraception for each of the following:
   a. Samir has a family, but knows he could not care properly for any more children. He can't have a permanent method as that would be changing what God has made.
   b. Jessica is married and wants no more children. Her religion does not agree with any artificial methods, and says permanent methods are against God's wishes.
   c. Xavier needs to protect his partner from a sexually transmitted infection (STI) that he carries making sure there is no exchange of body fluids during sex.
   d. Helena has asked for a foolproof form of contraception – one that would be 100 per cent safe.

Now you know about contraception

Religious attitudes to sexual matters

Buddhism

Ultimately, for Buddhists, **sexuality** has to be put aside. It is about desire and craving, which the Four Noble Truths explain we must stop if we want to achieve enlightenment.

Buddhism, in all its forms, has a very strong celibate tradition, with many monasteries and convents. The energy that might have been put into sexual activity is channelled into spiritual activity to try to reach enlightenment. Having said this, there are many lay Buddhists who live as families. Sex is seen as natural, but more rewarding as part of a loving, caring relationship, so chastity is encouraged. Couples should use contraception to limit their family size, and so practise responsible parenthood. This can also prevent the suffering of a new life that is forced to be born unwanted.

Buddhism encourages people to follow the Five Precepts, including the precept to avoid sexual immorality, including adultery. Breaking this precept will lead to suffering, causing bad karma. Karma is what determines the quality of the next life. It could also be said to break other Precepts because it will hurt others (First Precept), and will involve telling lies (Second Precept).

Buddhists do not condemn sex before marriage, or homosexuality, as long as it is part of a loving, caring relationship. Where sex is just based on lust, such as one-night stands, then this is craving, which is one of the 'Three Poisons'. In this case, it is unskilful living and could negatively affect future rebirths, but certainly keeps us in the cycle of samsara.

Christianity

Most Christians believe that only married couples should have sex, and only with each other. Chastity is a virtue. Attitudes to the use of contraception vary. There is a celibate tradition within Christianity – monastic life and the priesthood.

Every sexual act must be within the framework of marriage. The Roman Catholic Church teaches that only married couples should have sex, and the most important reason for sex is to have children. There should be a chance of pregnancy within every act of sex.

Any sex other than between husband and wife is wrong. Sex before marriage is called fornication, and is a sin. The same goes for masturbation because it can't lead to pregnancy. Using contraception is against Catholic teaching because it cancels out the chance of pregnancy. Most Catholics follow natural methods of contraception, though in Western countries this teaching is often ignored. Homosexual sex is thought to be unnatural and, again, can't lead to pregnancy, so it is also a sin and wrong. In places, the Bible also says it is wrong for a man to sleep with another man, for example, which has also been used to argue that homosexuality is wrong.

Some Christians tolerate sex before marriage in a relationship that is leading to marriage, seeing it as an expression of love. They also stress the need for responsible parenthood – only having as many children as you can properly look after. So the use of contraception is encouraged. Many Christians disagree with sterilisation (unless for medical reasons) because it is damaging what God has created.

The Bible says 'Do not commit adultery'; Jesus says that even to look at someone lustfully is wrong, so an affair is also wrong and a sin. Having an affair means that you break all the promises you made before God when marrying. Christians don't agree with **adultery**.

Task

Write out each of the words in blue. Give a definition for each. Then say what each religion you have studied says about it.

Hinduism ॐ

For a Hindu man, life is split into four ashramas or stages. Sexual relationships can only happen in the second stage, which is that of the married householder (*grihastha*). For the other three stages, the man should remain celibate. This means that women also have sexual relationships only within marriage. Sex before marriage and homosexuality are both against the religion. Sex is seen as a gift from the Ultimate Reality (God), and must be treated with care and **respect**. It is for enjoyment and to have children.

Chastity is important in Hinduism, and all are expected to be virgins before marriage, with their only partner ever being the person whom they marry. Two important Hindu virtues are self-discipline and respect, and adultery goes against both of these. Since adultery causes others to suffer, it brings bad karma to the adulterer, and negatively affects their rebirth.

Hindus do not object to using contraception, rather, they encourage it. Responsible parenthood is stressed, though the need for a son rather than a daughter to carry out certain religious rituals often leads to less use of contraception. During the year, though, there are many days when couples should avoid sex – **festivals**, full/new moon, holy days and others – up to 208 in total, and this obviously will act as a form of birth control.

Islam ☪

Islam does not agree with choosing never to marry or with monastic lifestyles. It is a religious duty to marry and have children. Every person should be a virgin before marriage, and observe chastity before and during marriage. Celibacy as a life choice is wrong.

If only those who are married have sex, then it is thought that society is protected because all the issues linked to sex outside marriage are gone. The message is very clear in Islam – only married couples may have sex, and then only with each other. Prophet Muhammad (pbuh) spoke of sex as being special within marriage. He said it was a source of pleasure and provided the blessing of children from God, if the couple so wished. This means that Muslims can and should use contraception. Muhammad (pbuh) also said that couples should only have as many children as they can properly look after – responsible parenthood.

The Qur'an sets out specific punishments for those who have sex before marriage, commit adultery, or have homosexual relationships. It calls these people fornicators, and punishment is severe – flogging if single, execution if married. This still happens today – for example, a woman was stoned to death in November 2008 in Somalia for adultery. In several places, the Qur'an specifically mentions adultery, always saying it is wrong: 'Do not commit adultery. It is shameful and an evil way to act' (Surah 17:32).

Task

1 Look at the names of the couples written on the wall. No couple is married. John and Sara only met last week, whereas the other two couples have been together for months or years. Explain what the attitude of each of your two religions would be to each couple having a sexual relationship.

2 a If John and Sara got married, what would be the attitude of each religion about them having sex?
  b What advice might be given by each religion about contraception?

3 If Zack and Carl had a Civil Partnership, what would the attitude of the religions be to their sexual relationship?

Judaism

The family is very important in Judaism. Anything that goes against this ideal is wrong. Marriage is highly recommended, whereas a life of celibacy is not. The Torah states that woman was made from man to be his companion. This is interpreted to mean marriage. A sex drive is healthy, and sex within marriage is for pleasure and having children.

The first command given to humans was to be fruitful and multiply, which is understood to mean having at least one boy and one girl. Different branches of Judaism have different attitudes to contraception. Orthodox Jews will accept it for medical/health reasons; they often use the Pill because it does not interfere in the actual act of sex, and does not directly cause the wasting of seed, which is forbidden in the Torah. Reform Jews accept contraception also for social/economic reasons, so use more forms. For all Jews, sex is forbidden at certain times within the menstrual cycle. This acts as a form of birth control.

The Torah lists punishments for sex before marriage, adultery and homosexuality, which are all considered to be wrong. Jews are expected to be virgins before marriage and observe chastity all their life. Committing adultery breaks one of the Ten Commandments, and carries the death penalty in the Torah even if that is never carried out.

Jewish law calls homosexuality an abomination. Orthodox Jews still believe this, though state that homosexuals should not be persecuted. Many Reform and Liberal Jews accept homosexuality if it is within a loving relationship.

Sikhism

Sexuality is seen as a gift from God, because all beings have sexual urges. However, Sikhs warn against being controlled by your sex drive, and believe it should be controlled by marriage. So sex before marriage is wrong, and Sikhs try to protect even against the temptation of it, for example, discouraging dancing with the opposite sex in case it leads to evil thoughts. In the Adi Granth, Sikhs are warned to avoid that which produces evil thoughts in the mind. Married life is seen as the norm – celibacy as a life choice isn't encouraged. Chastity, though, is a virtue and highly valued before and within marriage as a form of self-control. Although most Sikhs see homosexuality as wrong – a form of *haumai* or selfishness – some accept it as part of what God has created in a person.

In the wedding ceremony, Sikhs make promises including to be faithful. These promises are made in front of God. The Rahit Maryada forbids adultery, saying the touch of another man's wife is like a poisonous snake, and adultery is one of the Four Abstinences of Sikhism.

When it comes to deciding on which contraception to use, Sikhs can choose for themselves. They are encouraged to follow responsible parenthood – only having as many children as can be properly looked after. Sikhs would not use permanent forms of contraception though, except for medical reasons, because these change the body that God has given.

The Basics

Complete a copy of the table opposite for each of the two religions you are studying. Using a table in this way keeps your notes brief and easy to read later when you are revising. Obviously you'll need to leave more space in the table, especially in the final column.

Topic	Agree/disagree	Reasons why
a Celibacy		
b Chastity		
c Sex before marriage		
d Contraception		
e Adultery		
f Homosexuality		

Now you know about religious attitudes to sex

Marriage and the family

Marriage is the joining of two people as a legal couple. Done religiously, it is before God for God's blessing (**covenant**).

Why do people marry?

People marry for many reasons.

Work them out with a partner.

- Love.
- Money.
- Family expectations.
- Religious duty.
- To legitimise a child.
- For sex.
- For companionship.

Upbringing and **culture** have a big influence on the reasons people marry.

Who to marry?

Most people would say 'marry who you want'.

Is it always that simple though?

Sometimes marrying who you want to has a cost, especially if your family doesn't approve of the person who you want to marry.

Why might this make things difficult?

Religious people are taught to honour their family and to honour their religion. You might, then, expect a religious person to marry someone who their family approves of, and someone who shares their religion.

So, should you get your parents' approval of your choice, or should it be your acceptance of their choice?

Accepting someone of your parents' choosing is what we call an arranged marriage – the parents have found someone for their son/daughter. The two meet, whilst chaperoned, and then decide to go ahead or not with the marriage. Divorce is still less common in this kind of marriage than in love marriages. Most religious people in the West, especially outside the Hindu, Muslim and Sikh faiths, would feel that getting their parents' approval of their own choice was the better way.

Why the same religion?

Well, for Muslims, Jews and Sikhs it is traditional to marry someone of the same religion. But perhaps the major reason is that if you married someone of a different faith, there would be many clashes – beliefs and attitudes to name but two. Which religious building would host the wedding? Which **vows** would be taken? When the time came to have children which religion would they follow? In any religion, the believer believes theirs is the right way, so why would you marry someone who is following the wrong one?

Roles in marriage

We have all seen or heard people on TV taking their vows; every soap has at least one big wedding a year!

Can you think of the marriage vows or promises? How would you expect your spouse to behave when married – you will come up with the same set of ideas?

So, did you get them? Be faithful, love and cherish, give support in all situations (sickness, health and so on) until death.

In marriage, a couple promises each other, through vows/promises or through a **contract**, to be good to each other, to be faithful and to support each other through good and bad, until the marriage is ended by death. It is commonsense really. If you were setting up an agreement with someone about how you'd live the rest of your life together, you'd come up with the same promises.

Additionally, roles might include who keeps house (cooking and cleaning), who leads the upbringing of children, who earns money for the family. In our society, it is becoming more common for all these tasks to be shared by the man and the woman, and even for them to be reversed from what is seen as traditional.

Religions can be very traditional or very like the rest of society – there aren't any hard rules.

Alternatives to marriage

Not everyone marries, but they may still have a relationship with someone. So how does that work?

- Cohabitation is living together as if married. The couple have no marriage certificate. Not everyone feels the need to go through a ceremony.
- Civil marriage registration is done at a registry office and may include promises, but it isn't religious.
- Civil partnership is the legal registration of a same-sex couple. This means that in law they are treated as if married – they have all the legal protections that a married couple are entitled to.

Here is what some people said about these:

Me and my partner have lived together for fourteen years. We have two kids. Marriage is just a piece of paper, and we don't need that.

Dave

We married but we aren't religious, so we went to the registry office. It was a nice, quiet do – just right for our relationship. It gives us both protection if the relationship fails, but it also gives us benefits – such as tax advantages – whilst in the relationship.

Jay

We went through a civil partnership last year. As a gay couple, we were never going to be given the same rights as everyone else without this process. For example, now I am her next of kin – with all the rights that brings. I couldn't even have visited her in hospital without her family's consent before the civil partnership.

Lucy

I think that if a couple love each other, then marriage is the key. It is the only appropriate setting for sexual relationships and having children.

Jade

The Basics

1. Explain what is meant by 'marriage', 'cohabitation' and 'civil partnership'.
2. Why do people marry?
3. Explain the roles within marriage, including parenting.
4. **Marriage is old fashioned these days.** What do you think? Explain your answer.

Parenting

You have just seen that part of the reason for marriage and the roles within marriage is about children. So let's explore that a little.

Why do people have children? Are there any specifically religious reasons for having children?

Having children shows:

- **commitment**
- love
- fulfilment of a relationship
- duty
- family tradition.

You probably have more reasons, but these are the most common.

So what is religious parenting?

It is the same as any other **parenting** – it is looking after children and making sure that they get the best start to life. Most parents want the same or better chances for their children than they had. They want their children to be happy, well adjusted and ready to do well in their lives. Religious parents also want their children to follow their own faith, so they teach them its beliefs and how to practise it, for example, how to behave and how to worship. Many even put their child through an initiation ceremony for the faith (see pages 66–69).

For people who aren't religious, this might seem unfair – that the parents 'force' the religion on the child. However, think about it. They believe that this faith is right and that it is the key to happiness, if not in this life, then definitely in the next. They want what is best for their child and they believe that this is it. When you put it in those terms, passing on a faith is an act of great love.

Now you have thought about marriage

Marriage ceremonies

Buddhist wedding

Buddhism does not have a set ceremony for marriage, so the ceremonies are completely non-religious.

A couple will visit a monk to have their fortunes read and a lucky date is decided from that reading for their wedding.

June

Mon	Tue	Wed	Thur	Fri	Sat	Sun
				1	2	3
4	5	6	7	8	9	10
11	12	13	14	15	16	17
18	19	20	21	22	23	24
25	26	27	28	29	30	

Buddhists will follow the local customs of their country for marriage, which may include registering their marriage officially.

Later, the couple might visit the monastery or temple to invite a monk to bless their marriage. He does this by reciting verses from Buddhist scriptures. He also gives them advice about being a married Buddhist.

The couple might then invite the monk to a feast, as a sign of their thanks for his blessing.

Christian wedding

Marriage is a sacrament in some Christian traditions – it brings a blessing from God. Let's look at the Roman Catholic ceremony where marriage takes place as part of the Mass.

The couple will come to church to be united in marriage by the priest. He greets them before the whole congregation.

The priest then reads a homily – a speech about marriage and what Christian marriage is.

The priest asks three set questions to the bride and groom to make sure they understand the responsibilities of marriage.

The couple make their vows to each other.

FOR RICHER, FOR POORER

LOVE AND CHERISH

The priest declares that they have agreed to marry before God, and accepts their decision. It is at this point he says:

What God has joined together, let no man put asunder.

The rings are blessed and exchanged.

The priest blesses the marriage.

The couple sign the marriage register. This is the civil part of the ceremony.

Hindu wedding ॐ

Find out all about Hindu marriages at www.vivaaha.org.

The wedding ceremony is part of a whole set of ceremonies, which lead up to and continue after the actual ceremony. We will concentrate on the ceremony.

The groom, his family and friends arrive for the wedding to be received by the bride's family.

Under a specially-built canopy, the priest begins the ceremony with a blessing on the couple. The bride and groom give each other garlands.

The father pours out sacred water to show he gives away his daughter, whilst the priest recites hymns from the Vedas. The groom also accepts his duties and responsibilities as a husband.

The bride and groom face each other. The end of her scarf is tied to his shirt to symbolise their eternal union. They exchange their rings.

Holding hands, the couple throw samagree – a mix of sandalwood, herbs, sugar, rice and ghee – into the sacred fire to ask for the deities' blessing on their marriage.

The bride and groom walk three times around the fire, reciting hymns and prayers.

At the end of each circuit of the fire, they both step on to a stone to pray that their marriage will be strong like the stone.

They then take seven steps around the fire and, with each, make a wedding promise such as:

To share joys and sorrows

The ceremony ends with a prayer that the marriage cannot be broken.

Muslim wedding 

Traditionally, Muslim marriage ceremonies last up to five days, because of many cultural traditions depending upon which Muslim country or area is involved. We will concentrate on the actual wedding ceremony itself.

The ceremony, which would take place on day four of a five-day celebration, is called nikkah. It is always a simple ceremony and may be performed by an imam. Most nikkah are performed at the home of the bride or groom and not the mosque.

The groom has to declare a mahr – a dowry, showing his respect for her. It can include anything she has asked for – money, clothes, even a house. The groom can pay this over time and is not allowed to take it away – it is hers. It is the first part – a second, equal part is given if divorce occurs.

An imam usually leads the ceremony, but it could be any respected male. The bride does not have to be there – she will have given her consent beforehand.

Some couples take vows. They will have signed marriage contracts beforehand about what they expect from the marriage and what the rights of their partner will be.

The imam announces the couple's intention to marry and asks if anyone has any objections. He also recites some verses from the Qur'an and the Nikkah Khutba, which are about the purpose of marriage.

3 The consent of the bride is asked for three times by the imam. After it is given, the marriage is complete.

Jewish wedding 

Jewish weddings begin with the signing of the Ketubah (marriage contract) in front of four witnesses. It details the legal terms of the marriage.

The bridegroom places a veil over the bride's face, to show that he will protect and look after his wife.

The bride and groom go to the huppah (wedding canopy), where the bride walks around the groom up to seven times.

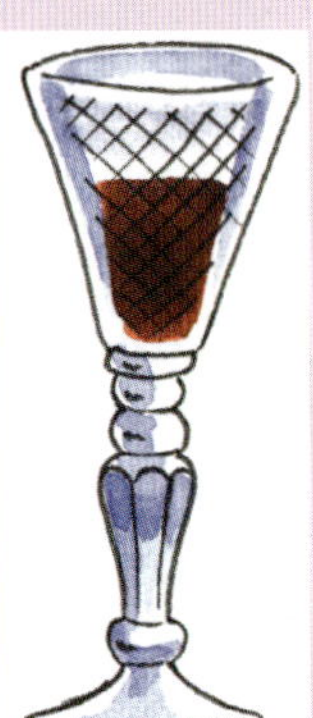

The couple drink a glass of wine – the first of seven to represent the seven days of creation and the start of the building of a marriage.

A ring is given to the bride or rings are exchanged. Ring(s) must be an undecorated, unbroken circle, showing the hope for a harmonious marriage.

The rabbi makes a speech about the responsibilities of marriage and about the couple. Prayers are said. The cantor sings.

Finally, the groom crushes a glass under his foot to remember the destruction of the temple, but also to hope that bad luck will not come to the marriage. There is a tradition that a wicked spirit visits each wedding to cause trouble. Breaking the glass gives it the trouble it looked for. With this act, the marriage is complete.

Sikh wedding 

Check out www.sikhs.org/wedding for more details and pictures.

A Sikh marriage is called Anand Karaj. Only Sikhs can have this ceremony. Anyone who is a full Khalsa Sikh can lead the ceremony.

The groom listens to kirtan in the gurdwara as he waits for his bride to arrive. When she arrives, she sits on his left in front of the Guru Granth Sahib. The Ardas prayer will be said to begin the ceremony. This prayer begins and ends all ceremonies.

The end of the groom's scarf is placed in the hands of the bride, whilst four lavan (verses of a hymn written by the fourth Guru) from the Guru Granth Sahib are read.

When the second lavan is reached, the couple stand and, groom first, walk slowly around the Guru Granth Sahib. They do this for each lavan.

The ragis read out the Anand Sahib and a randomly chosen hymn from the Guru Granth Sahib is read out.

The ceremony ends with the Ardas prayer, and the distribution of karah parshad (blessed food) to all.

Research Task

Find more details and pictures to illustrate your own descriptions of the marriage ceremonies.

The website www.bbc.co.uk has a great religion section with good details and pictures of all the ceremonies, as well as links to other useful websites and lots of information about attitudes to marriage.

Now you know about marriage ceremonies

Divorce

Many marriages face difficulties. A number of those will fail and be legally dissolved – this is what we mean by the term divorce. In the UK, more than one in three first marriages ends in divorce.

Why do marriages fail? Can you think of some reasons?

Any difficulties in a marriage can put strain on it – money, arguments, different attitudes or beliefs, affairs, illness, job issues or abuse. When these difficulties become too great for one or both to cope with, the couple might turn to divorce as a solution. Divorce becomes more manageable than the marriage.

Should it be easy to get a divorce?

Religious people might think that divorce is always wrong. Many of them do see a need for divorce, but feel that it should not be an easy option, because that would encourage people to not even try at their marriage. In 1969, the Church of England played a key role in getting the divorce laws relaxed, which has eventually led to more divorces. Religions argue that people made a very serious commitment by getting married, so should work hard at their marriage, and even harder when it is in difficulty. Only as a last option should they use divorce.

Support for marriages in difficulty

Since divorce is not a welcome option, religions try to support couples in their times of difficulty. Obviously, families will support them – look after the children, listen and help them problem solve, and so on. Religious people will also do these things, but they might also encourage the couple through their religion – through prayer, reading their holy books, and so on. Our society also provides marriage counselling **services**.

Buddhism

Any vows made are serious and so an agreement to marry is a serious commitment, which should not be broken easily. Since marriage is seen as a thing that keeps society stable, in Buddhist countries divorce is discouraged. It is not against Buddhist teachings though.

Buddhism teaches:

- Keep the Five Precepts.
- Be compassionate.
- Thoughts, deeds and actions should always be positive, because they have a karmic value that shapes our next lifetime(s).

For Buddhists, sometimes divorce has to be seen as the right option. Two people are causing themselves and others great suffering by staying together. This breaks precepts, creates bad karma and goes against Buddhist principles of compassion and ahimsa.

Christianity

For Roman Catholics, divorce is always wrong. Marriage is a sacrament that cannot be broken. Promises are made to God and each other to stay together 'until death do us part' and these promises are binding.

For most other Christians, divorce is discouraged, but accepted as a last resort. It is sometimes the lesser of two evils, and also a **necessary evil**.

Christianity teaches:

- God hates divorce – Old Testament.
- Whoever divorces…then marries another; it is as if he committed adultery – Jesus.
- Forgiveness and love – Jesus.

The Basics

1. Explain what is meant by divorce.
2. Give reasons why couples divorce.
3. Explain the attitude of religious believers to problems in marriage and divorce.
4. **Divorce is always wrong**. Do you agree?

Now you know about divorce

Hinduism

Hindu law forbids divorce to the Brahmin caste, but it is available to all others. It does happen throughout Hindu society, but is frowned upon.

Hinduism teaches:

- 'I promise never to abandon her, whatever happens' – wedding vow.
- Marriage is one of the spiritual stages in life.
- Divorce is granted for specific reasons – Hindu Marriage Act (1955) and Manusmriti scriptures.

The Manusmriti scriptures said that a man could replace any wife who was quarrelsome or difficult; the law allows for divorce in the case of cruelty, non-production of children and other reasons. Clearly, divorce is both available and within the religious teachings, however, it is not a common event. There is a great stigma over divorce, and it is especially difficult for women who have been divorced. Couples tend to stay together because of these pressures.

Judaism

Marriage is a sacred commitment and union. Although divorce is allowed, it is as a last resort.

Judaism teaches:

- G-d hates divorce – Nevi'im.
- When a man puts aside the wife of his youth, even the very altar weeps – Talmud.
- A court can grant a woman divorce if she can show that she can no longer live with him – Maimonides.

Technically, it is easy to get a divorce is Judaism. However, it is not desirable and every effort will be made to help the couple stay together. Before any divorce can be given, a period of time has to pass that allows attempts at reconciliation. Then the husband will serve the bill of divorce (get) – because he put forward the original contract with its promises, so it is he who cancels it. The get is written in black ink with no mistakes and on parchment. It is an official document and is served before the Beth Din (Jewish Court of Law). Then the marriage is ended.

Islam

Divorce is available to both men and women, however, it is seen as the absolute last resort. Much work has to have gone into trying to make the marriage work.

Islam teaches:

- Of all legal things, the one Allah most hates is divorce – Qur'an.
- Marry and do not divorce; the throne of Allah shakes due to divorce – Hadith.
- If you fear a breach between a man and his wife, appoint two arbiters – Qur'an.

A Muslim couple and their families are expected to work hard to fix any problems in a marriage to avoid divorce. There has to be mediation between them and they have to give time for reflection and to solve problems. If divorce is still the solution, then the man states 'I divorce you' three times before witnesses. He must then wait three months – to be sure his wife is not pregnant, and perhaps try to resolve the problems. After that, he must pay the second part of the dowry to show the marriage is ended.

Sikhism

Divorce is not the Sikh way, but is accepted by the faith. Marriage should be a lifetime commitment and worked at, especially when times are difficult.

Sikhism teaches:

- Marriage is a sacrament.
- Marriage is the union of two souls and a lifelong commitment.
- If the husband and wife dispute, their concern for their children should reunite them – Adi Granth.

If a marriage is in difficulty, both families will try to help solve the problems – after all, given this was an arranged marriage, its collapse reflects badly on the families as well as the couple. Divorce carries a stigma and is avoided if possible. Of course, Sikhs accept that, at times, a couple have no other choice, but it must be their choice to divorce – it is a matter for a person's individual **conscience.**

Exam practice – revising the details

These are revision styles that worked for these young people. Perhaps they will work for you.

Our teacher pointed out that religions have a set of fundamental ideas. So I learnt those key ideas and applied them every time to my questions. It didn't give me full marks for a question – I had to learn some specifics for that! It did give me a really good start, which got me over half marks every time. So 'Love your neighbour' counts for attitudes to your family and partner and children, as well as just about anything that involves someone else – the list goes on and on (but my revision didn't need to!)

Emma

Pictures help me, and pictures with labels help me even more, rather than just words alone. Get pictures of as many of the things you study as you can. Then you can think of the images in the exam and they will help you remember. For example, a wedding picture with notes about the ceremony, why people marry, their roles and so on written around the outside.

Carlton

I made a set of flashcards and got someone to test my knowledge regularly using them. Put images and words on to the cards, such as words to define, or religious ideas to link to marriage. Someone shows you one flashcard and you talk about it. I even got my mum to help – so she knew I was revising!

Jack

When we did tests, before she marked them, our teacher went through them with us telling her what we should have put. She got us to tell her the answers as a class, and then told us what an examiner would be looking for. We had to guess at our mark and grade for the test. It really sharpened up my understanding of how to answer questions and made me read my answers properly – I never did that before when I got tests back. This all helped me learn from my mistakes and improve my exam performance.

Ronnie

I liked doing tests – they made me revise in bits and helped me to get used to all the questions I'd see and improve my timing. Sounds a bit weird that, but it is all true. Our teacher gave us a test after every topic – if you revise properly each time, it makes mock revision and final revision miles easier.

Toni

I spaced all I knew over a page – called a thought map. You put the topic in the middle, then surround it with information about that topic. Small details are further out from the middle, and you group the ideas by what they tell you about the topic. I used colour to split the groups, and added pictures too. Helped me remember loads, and I did them for every subject not just RE.

Samira

I went back over my answers and read them to find what I did worng. I wrote tips to improve them based on the techniques my teacher showed us. Then I used the tips to write perfect answers.

Gemma

Topic Two Religion, sport and leisure

This topic thinks about religions' attitudes to **healthy living**, and especially to sport and **leisure**. You will need to know why we take part in sport, how it is good for us, attitudes to winning, how sport can be like religion in some ways and the moral issues met within sports.

What do we mean by leisure time?

Leisure, or free time, is the time spent not working or doing chores. It is also the time before or after necessary activities such as eating and sleeping, working or running a **business**, attending school and doing homework and household chores.

The difference between leisure and compulsory activities isn't clear because some people have jobs that others think of as leisure. For example, an activity counts as 'leisure' when we choose to do it, we feel motivated by it, and it gives us a sense of well-being.

The idea of leisure time is thought to have begun in Victorian Britain in the late-nineteenth century. In early factories, people worked up to eighteen hours per day, with Sundays off. By the 1870s, though, more efficient machinery and the **trade unions** meant a reduction in working hours per day, and Saturdays, as well as Sundays, off work.

As workers used their wages for leisure activities, the modern entertainment industry began to appear. This Victorian concept – the weekend – saw the beginning of leisure time as it is known today.

'What is this life if, full of care,
We have no time to stand and stare…'

'Leisure' by W. H. Davies

Types of leisure

If you work indoors and spend most of your time sitting down, you might do some physical activity or sports during your leisure time. If your job involves a lot of physical activity, you may prefer to spend your free time doing quiet, relaxing activities.

Most people like socialising with friends. For many, having a regular night out is part of their free time, whether it is joining friends in a pub, watching a film, playing games or dancing the night away at a club.

Some people do leisure activities that have a long-term goal (for example, volunteer paramedics who hope to eventually become professional paramedics).

Many people also study in the evenings, both for interest and to help their **career** prospects.

For some people, religion is a key part of their leisure time.

Discussion Time

- Why is leisure time important?
- Do different cultures have different types of leisure activities? Why?
- 'One person's chosen leisure activity might be another's hell!' What do you think?
- Should our leisure activities be useful and purposeful?

So, let's ask the question...

What do we get out of this leisure time?

There is so much out there for us to do. The leisure industry is worth billions of pounds, so there must be many reasons as to why we do it. Of course, this will depend upon the activity we are doing. Many of us do more than one activity and therefore we gain more benefits.

Task

1. Think about two leisure activities that you do. What benefits to your life do you get from each one? Explain how.
2. a. Below are some examples of leisure activities. Using some of the ideas in the spider diagram, explain what the benefits are for each activity. (Also try to think of some different benefits to those shown in the spider diagram.)

   b. Which activities would religious people consider to be good for us? Why?

Playing football | Fishing | Going to the pub | Studying

Watching a film | Walking | Church fête

Doing yoga | Playing squash | Going to the gym | Collecting stamps

Misuse of leisure time

As well as being very good for us, it could be said that there are many people who do not use their leisure time in a purposeful way. An activity that can be really good for one person might be detrimental to another.

Can you think of examples and explain why/how?

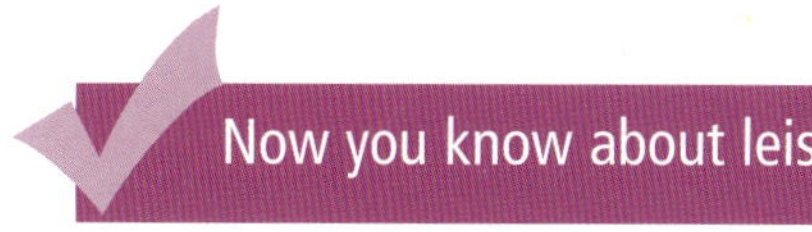

Morality in sport

This is a major concern in all sports today. Success in most sports can lead to riches and fame far beyond what could ever be imagined. This has led many people to 'bend the rules' as far as possible to be able to win as much as they can. For many, 'winning at all costs' is now their guiding principle in their chosen sport.

Do I compete honestly?

Is **fair competition** important?

Am I willing to use drugs?

Is winning more important than participation?

Let's think about this in relation to sport today. At school, we are often told that when we do sport 'it's not the winning that matters, it's the taking part'. In the real world, few professionals play just for the love of the game.

The world is a competitive place and when seconds make the difference between winning and losing, when a point dropped could cost a team millions of pounds, when no one remembers who came second, when winning could be a life-changing experience and set you up for life, the temptation to cheat and enhance performance is understandably there.

Task

Divide the class into four groups. Two groups choose Statement 1 below; the other two groups choose Statement 2. Out of the two groups for each statement, one chooses to be for and the other against. Groups either create a poster or organise a debate.

Statement 1: 'All athletes should have the motto to "win at all costs"'.

Statement 2: 'It is hard not to be tempted to take PEDs.'

The debate	The issues
Fair competition Honesty is key. It is important that training and competing are done fairly. If someone wins a race or a competition, then it is important that the win is done so by merit. The best person with the most/best ability should win. Upsets do happen, people can have off days or outperform expectations, but people should play by the rules. If a person somehow cheats, it undermines everything.	• A cheat who wins makes a mockery of the competition. • Fellow competitors who have worked hard lose out, as do fellow team members. • Crowds/fans are let down by people they often worship as heroes. • Medals are lost and competitors banned for life and their reputation is shattered.
Performance-enhancing drugs (PEDs) Most commonly used are steroids. They allow a sportsperson to train harder and push their bodies to a level that non-users can't reach. PEDs are taken before competitions start to improve muscle mass, as a stimulant to increase alertness, for painkiller use, as a sedative to calm nerves, as a diuretic to lose weight, or as a masking drug to hide other drugs taken. Many sports now have regular drug testing as the pressure to win becomes greater. Cycling, weightlifting and sprinting have all been hit by major names being found guilty of drug use.	• The right person has not won the race/competition. • The person is risking severe health problems (even early death). • In certain sports, body building is essential – drug use allows unnatural muscle mass. • It gives the drug user a massive advantage over fellow competitors – they become more focused, more aggressive, stronger, calmer, able to train through injuries, etc.

Now you know about morality in sport

Religious attitudes to morality in sport

Buddhism

We could apply right action, right intention, right view, etc to this topic. These suggest that competition should be fair, equal and participated in for the right reasons. Any cheating would be considered wrong and would have karmic consequences. Unwholesome acts (akusala) will affect rebirth. One of the Five Precepts is to not harm the body with drugs.

Islam

Whilst cricket is popular, Muslim participation in great numbers in many sports is just developing. Competitors are bound by Islamic ethics. Allah knows all our thoughts and actions and we will be judged on the Day of Judgement. We should use the talents that Allah has given us and, as honesty is a key virtue, cheating is unethical. Winning correctly through hard work and training glorifies Allah. Drugs are haram and, therefore, we should not use them as this also separates us from Allah.

Christianity

Christianity stresses that people should live and work in a disciplined way – proper behaviour in sport is exactly this. Through sport, life values are learnt – honesty, integrity and fair play

- '...your body is the temple of the Holy Spirit' (1 Corinthians 6:19).
- 'Everyone must submit himself to the governing authorities, for there is no authority except that which God has established' (Romans 13:1).

Judaism

'Keeping the body healthy and fit is part of serving G-d, a person should avoid whatever undermines bodily health' (Maimonides). Jews believe that drug use alters mental states, causes loss of self-control and, as a person does not own their body, they should not damage it. No great emphasis is put on sport, but where it is played it should be done with honesty and integrity. Our body is from G-d and, as such, we should respect it (Genesis).

Hinduism

Hinduism tells us life should be pure – no bad thoughts or habits. We should serve others, as they reflect God. We are all linked as if in kinship. We should not deceive ourselves or others. All of these can be applied to fair play in sport. Hindus also follow the Golden Rule – so to cheat others breaks that.

Sikhism

Sikhs put great emphasis on physical fitness – many were soldiers and warriors. Sikhism says that truth is the foremost, but higher than truth is truthful living – cheating would not fulfil this. Sewa is a key action and, if you are being dishonest to others, then it is not being done. Cheating would be seen as a selfish desire (haumai) which is wrong. Harmful substances like drugs go against the principles of Sikhism. Since Sikhs should fight injustice, sports cheating would be wrong

Task

Explain the attitude of the religion(s) to cheating in sport.

Now you know religious attitudes

Money, money, money...

John Terry (Chelsea FC)

Cristiano Ronaldo (Man Utd)

Rafael Nadal (Wimbledon Champion)

David Beckham (LA Galaxy)

Lewis Hamilton (F1 Racing Driver)

Do you recognise these names? Of course you do! These people appear regularly on our TV screens. But what do they all have in common? Well, they are all very successful in their jobs, all very talented, all have reached the top and all are recognised as the best in their sport: two England captains, one World Player of the Year, one Wimbledon Champion, one F1 Driving Champion. However, it's not these things that are the issue – money is! They each earn massive salaries – over £1m a year. On top of this, they have very lucrative sponsorship deals and many of the top stars earn more through sponsorship than they do for actually performing in their chosen area. Think of Brand Beckham for example.

David Beckham

The Basics

1 Why do you think sports pay 'superstar' wages?
2 What problems do people have with 'superstar' wages?
3 **Money in sport has got out of hand**. What do you think? Explain your opinion.
4 **Superstar salaries are too much**. Explain what religious people would think about this statement.

Now you know about payment of superstars

Money has become a key part of sport. Some would say that it has ruined sport. Do people now play for the money or for the love of the game – as it should be? Top football players want contracts of £150,000 per week; the Shanghai Tennis Masters offers prize money of £1m; cricketers in the Indian Premier League 20/20 are offered contracts way beyond their dreams; and the England Cricket Team played in the Stanford Challenge in the Caribbean for £1m each. So where does this type of prize money come from? The answer is us! So many of us watch it – buy expensive tickets, buy merchandise, pay for TV coverage – that the companies want to use people to advertise their products. We want to see the best and therefore sports stars can command high wages. To be at the top, teams need the top stars and, for this, they have to be able to pay a lot.

Lewis Hamilton

Religious people argue that the money issue has got out of hand – some would call it obscene. Some would say that no one is worth that sort of money. People have become greedy, and sport encourages this. For example, is £120,000 not enough for Manchester United to pay Ronaldo per week? In 2008, it was suggested that Ronaldo's agent argued that if United wanted to keep him, they should hit the £150,000 per week mark.

How does sponsorship work?

Sponsorship is an advertising tool. Companies invest money in sporting areas hoping to get people to buy their brands. It can be seen in many different ways. It could be an individual being paid to wear certain brands of clothing or use certain makes of equipment. It could be of a team, so that the company's name is used on merchandise as advertising, for example, Carlsberg sponsor Liverpool FC. It could also be a sports star advertising a product. Sponsorship works in two ways:

1 The company hopes that if their name appears on products attached to famous people/teams, etc., then people will be persuaded to switch to buying their products.
2 The money from sponsorship helps the individuals/teams compete at the highest level.

AIG (Man Utd)	£56.5m	Four years
Barclays (English Premiership)	£65.8m	Four years
Carlsberg (Liverpool FC)	£22m	Three years
Nike (Tiger Woods)	$87m	Ongoing
Beijing Olympics 2008	Ten major companies paid $850m (combined) to sponsor the Games – Coca-Cola, for example	Three-week competition

Money gained through sponsorship, 2008

Of course, we must remember that, although many people believe far too much money is spent on sponsorship, it does have its advantages. Without sponsorship, many athletes would not be able to participate because the money enables them to train and buy necessary equipment. Barcelona FC and Rangers FC have allowed their shirts to be used by the charity UNICEF without any payment, so they are using the power of normal sponsorship advertising to hopefully get people to donate to this charity.

Gambling

Gambling has become a major part of sporting activities. For those who watch sport, it appears to make it more interesting if money is at stake. It might just be a bit of fun – first scorer, half-time and full-time results, winner of a tournament, top scorer, etc. For others, there is serious money involved, for example, in horse racing. There is great concern amongst religious groups about how gambling is becoming a problem for families where more money is spent on this addiction than can actually be afforded.

Task

1 Explain what is meant by sponsorship.
2 How does gambling work in relation to sport?
3 How might religious people respond to the three situations described in the speech bubbles? Explain your answers.

I'm a premiership footballer. I'm actually one of the best. My salary is £120,000 per week and I've just agreed a deal with a well-known international company to wear their boots. They will pay me £3m a season.

I'm 16 and people say that I'm good enough to win a gold medal at the next Olympics. Show jumping is my sport. My horse is sponsored, so I'm able to look after him and transport him around the world. I need sponsorship if I am to be the best.

I'm 25, married with two children. I really like gambling – on almost anything really. Football on a Saturday, but the horses are my real thing. I visit the bookies every day – it's the buzz of the win. I do lose more than I win. We just do without stuff at home!

Now you know all about money issues in sport/leisure

Devotion

Many sports now have fanatical followers. Read the following information.

Name: Katie Smith

Age: 24

Occupation: Supply Teacher. I am a maths specialist and also do one-to-one tuition for exams.

Interests: All sports. I'm an Arsenal fan, but my big love is cricket.

About yourself: I've always been keen on sport. My dad was a PE teacher and he spent tons of time when I was young playing all kinds of games with me. On a Saturday, we always went to Highbury to watch Arsenal – we travelled home and away. As I grew up, cricket became my key interest. I always go the test matches in the summer here. The test match at Lords is like a pilgrimage for me – the hairs on my neck stand up as we wait for the start. I have all the kits – the white test shirt, the red and blue one-day kit and I'm an official member of the 'Barmy Army'. I work for six months a year, save as much as I can and then for the other six months I go on tour with England – the Caribbean, Australia, India, South Africa, Pakistan, Sri Lanka, New Zealand – I've been all over the world. I usually stay in the team hotel too. At home, I have signed framed pictures on my wall – my prize possession is a picture of Michael Vaughan holding the Ashes urn. The pictures go up both sides of my stairs – I guess you could say it is a bit like a shrine.

Task

1 Using the example of the cricket fan, explain how devotion in sport can be shown.
2 Why does Katie see her visit to Lords as a pilgrimage?
3 Look at the Liverpool FC photos. How could supporting a football team be said to be an example of worship?
4 a Use the internet to find the lyrics of 'You'll never walk alone'.
   b Could this be a religious song? Why?
   c What is the message in this song?
5 Look at the photo of the Kop. How might it be called a shrine?
6 Could a person make a pilgrimage to a place like Anfield?

'What would the world be like without football? Football has saved lives – soldiers have taken off in wars, put down their guns and played football. It has made Princes of paupers; it has given hope to the hopeless and brought smiles to the faces of the depressed. It has given something to those who had nothing... That's football! It's a wonderful game, there's nothing like it' Bill Shankly

(*Bernard, B. (1996)* The Shankly Legacy, *Breedon Books)*

Walk on, walk on, with hope in your heart, for you'll never walk alone, you'll never walk alone.

Now you know about devotion in sport

Is sport the new religion?

With words like 'worship', 'hymns', 'devotion', 'shrines', 'followers' and 'pilgrimage', people have asked the question as to whether sport has indeed become a religion. Numbers of people attending church worship, for example, are declining, yet football attendances and participation in many sporting areas are rising. Even the word 'spirituality' has been used. When asked about the spectators at Anfield, Bill Shankly (Liverpool Manager in the 1960s and 70s) answered, 'I think it is more than fanaticism. It's a religion with them. The thousands who come here to worship … it's a sort of shrine … Not just a football ground.'

So what do we need for a religion? A focus for worship, a leader, a set of beliefs, rules for behaviour, a shrine or building, a symbol, rituals and special days and a dress code.

Does sport have these things? Take the three major sports in Britain – football, rugby and cricket. Do a comparison – do they have all/most of the above? Explain how/why.

If we look a little deeper at the qualities that religion encourages, we can also find similarities here. God wants your allegiance in good times and bad…so do teams; both encourage support for God/team and each other; they both have rituals that they believe mystically aid the cause; and stories and music are written as hymns/songs to use in worship. These make you feel closer to God/the players. There is a feeling of togetherness and community. When walking into the building, there is a special feeling deep down inside the follower, one that you cannot always explain – but there is nothing like it!

When I go to watch my team, I make all the same preparations – I must be dressed properly, you see. It shows I belong and I respect the team. Everyone knows what I stand for when they see me dressed like this.

When we sing our hymn at the start of the game, everyone joins in and it is sung with real feeling. It's like being in a choir. We aim to praise and glorify our heroes. No one talks or is disrespectful – we feel like we are honouring those we worship and those who have gone before us.

The building itself is like a shrine. We decorate it with flags that tell the story of our history – a bit like stained-glass windows do in a church. There is one end of the stadium that is very special – a bit like an altar. It's where those with the most commitment stand and lead the worship throughout the game.

When we are watching the team, we show our adoration of them. We praise them to encourage them – we are all united together aiming for one goal. We chant their names – they know we love them for what they do for us. Our encouragement gives them energy and support to conquer the difficulties they are presented with during the game.

Task

1 Read the four statements above from the sports fans. For each one, explain:
   a why their views could be used to support the idea that sport is seen as a religion
   b why religious believers would not agree.

Now you know about religion in sport

Religion working through sport

In the UK, 2008 figures suggest that sport is a growing industry. Over 45 per cent of adults and 87 per cent of young people regularly participate in sport. The government is keen to increase these numbers by 2020. In comparison, only around 8 per cent of people attend church. However, no doubt there are very religious people who do play sport. Some people believe that God is with them during sporting activities. Often, before entering the field of play, we see people sign their chest with the sign of the cross, or look up towards heaven when they have won something.

The mission statement of Christians in Sport is reaching the world of sport for Christ. This is achieved by helping Christian players to:

1 **Pray** for their sporting friends.
2 **Play** in a way that honours God.
3 **Say** something of the Good News of Jesus Christ.

Being a Christian in sport affects the way that people train, play the game and generally lead their lives. Fair play is key to training and, during the game, people feel that they should be seen as a good example: '…let your light shine before men that they may see your good deeds and praise your Father in heaven' (Matthew 5:16).

Many people in sport these days are wealthy and how they spend their money is important. Sport provides social times, but this should not mean excessive drinking, drugs, sex, or not looking after yourself so that you let team mates down. They should be a reflection of God in all aspects of their lives. If God gave them their talents, then they should worship Him in the way that they are used.

Although other religions don't have formal organisations, this does not mean that for members of these faiths their religion is any less important. We see Muslim cricketers, for example, bow in submission to Allah on the pitch after scoring a hundred. So personal faith does affect attitude and approach to sporting activity.

Chaplains

A chaplain is a religious leader who works within an organisation. Over 70 per cent of professional sports teams in the UK now have chaplains. All the national football bodies, such as the FA and PFA, support this work.

The chaplaincy is a people role, and chaplains are involved with staff, management, directors and fans, as well as the youth and professional players.

The chaplain is easily accessible and helps in many of the areas others in the club can't – whether in an informal situation, as a listening ear, a friend or mentor. The chaplain also helps the club be involved in the local community. It isn't primarily a religious position, but chaplains can also be asked to do specifically religious things, such as pray for people or to officiate at occasions like weddings and funerals. They can also recommend support contacts from other denominations or faiths.

'Chaplains can be of help to all sorts of people involved with sport, when crisis, need, or difficulty comes.' (Sir Alex Ferguson, CBE, Manager, Man Utd)

'Our experience of chaplaincy has been uplifting…it has added a new and extremely important dimension to management and welfare.' (Bolton Wanderers FC)

'Our club chaplain has performed a very valuable service at the club. For players, he almost acts as a mentor. With the rest of the staff, he has offered real support for those who have suffered bereavement or just need someone to talk to. In today's helter-skelter world, a voice of calmness can be inspiring and invigorating.' (Lancashire County Cricket Club)

'Chaplaincy gives a whole other dimension to our club. It brings a personal touch – people feel like they can be listened to as individuals. If chaplaincy was established in every club, I think it would be of huge benefit to the game as a whole.' (Head Coach, British Lions Rugby Union)

Task

Use information on this page and the internet. Design a poster promoting either Religion in Sport or Chaplains in Sport.

Now you know about Christians in Sport

When being religious conflicts with competition

'God blessed the seventh day and made it holy.'
(Genesis 2:3)

'The Lord is my rock, my fortress and my deliverer;
My God, my strength, in whom I will trust.'
(Psalm 18)

Eric Liddell

Jonathan Edwards

Both of these athletes competed at the highest level of their chosen sports. However, their religious beliefs about their holy day caused problems. Liddell refused to compete in the 1924 Paris Olympics in the 100m – the event that he was favourite to win. Later, in 1991, Jonathan Edwards refused to compete in the World Championship Triple Jump. To him, it was wrong to compete on the **Sabbath** – the day when Christians should devote their time to worshipping God. In 1993, Edwards changed his position saying that God had told him through a dream to make full use of his ability, even if it meant competing on a Sunday. Michael Jones, the All Blacks rugby star, refused to play on Sundays. He missed three key games for the All Blacks in 1991.

To these top athletes, observing God's rules was more important than competing in the competition that they had trained for and they were willing to risk the loss of medals or trophies.

In other religions there are issues similar to this. For Muslims, Ramadan is a holy month and at times it clashes with sporting events. During Ramadan, Muslim athletes are at a disadvantage as they are expected to fast from sunrise to sunset. In 2012, Ramadan will take place from 21 July to 20 August, while the Olympics run from 27 July to 12 August. An anticipated 3000 Muslim competitors are expected to be affected. Although for Muslims this will cause problems, it is slightly different from the issue of Sunday competition. Sunday is instructed as a day of rest, whereas Ramadan is meant to be a test from Allah. The tougher the test, the greater reward!

However, it is an example of where religious observance can cause conflict with sport and leisure. In Judaism, **Shabbat** on a Saturday stops many children from joining in sport in a multicultural way. They often find that they have to set up separate leagues on different days because Saturday competition is not possible.

Task

1 Think about the statements shown in the spider diagram below.
   a How would you respond?
   b How do you think religious people would respond?

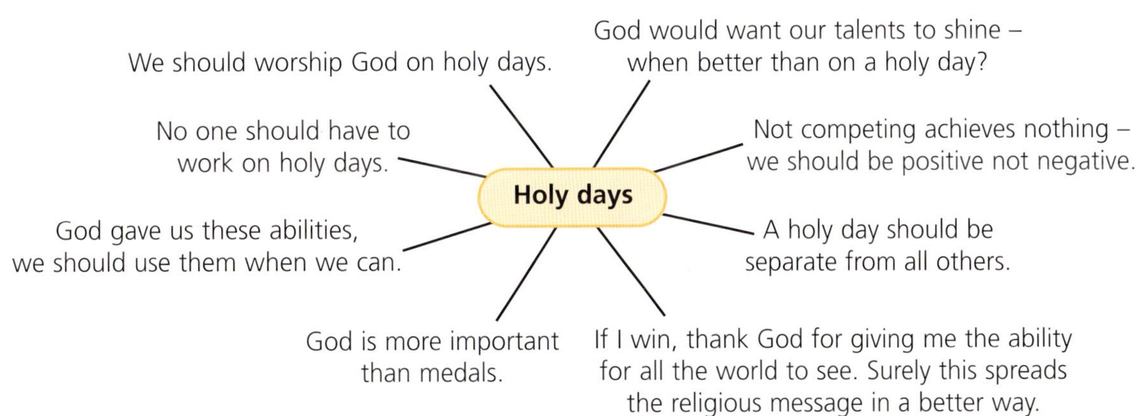

Where does skill and ability come from?

Is it natural or not? Are we born with it or do we learn it? Is it from God or elsewhere? Why do some of us have it and others don't? Interesting questions, eh? But can we answer them to any satisfaction?

The answer probably lies in a combination of all of these options. Let's look at the examples below:

Mozart was five years old when he produced his first composition 'Andante in C' in 1761. This cannot just be a result of learning or practice. He had to be born with this talent.

In 2009 Usain Bolt was the fastest man on earth – 2008 Olympic Gold medallist in the 100m. This could be a result of practice, but is the man naturally talented as well? His physical build makes his speed possible. Was this God-given or has the training he has done allowed his body to develop like this?

Michael Phelps won eight Gold medals at the Beijing Olympics, 2008. This had never been achieved before. He is the fastest man in the pool – known as the 'Baltimore Bullet'. Again, his physical build makes what he does possible. Was he born with this talent and has his potential been realised through training?

Muttiah Muralitharan – the greatest ever Sri Lankan spin bowler. He has a defect in his elbow that allowed him to bowl in a way no one else can. Was he born for this purpose? Without practice to develop his bowling style, the famous 'Doosra', he wouldn't have achieved what he has done.

Cristiano Ronaldo – it has been said he kicks a ball like no one else ever has. Does he have natural ability? Was he born with it and the desire to practise, practise and practise to get better? He spends longer on the training ground than anyone else at Man Utd. But…without that ability would practice make any difference?

These five people undoubtedly have 'ability' and 'talent'. So what do you think? You need to be able to formulate your own opinion and be able to justify it for the exam. You can use examples in your answers too. There are no right or wrong answers with this one – as long as your answer is sensible, then credit will be given.

The Basics

1. Where do you think you get your abilities and talents from?
2. Do you have to have natural talent to be very good at something?
3. **It's no use having natural ability unless you practise**. What do you think?
4. To what extent do you need talent, opportunity and the desire to practise to be really successful?
5. What would be a religious believer's response to this issue? Explain why.

Born with it

Ability

Learn it

Talent

Opportunity

Practice

Training

God

Now you have thought about where skill and ability come from

Sport – professional v. amateur

Organised sport began in the nineteenth century, mainly in the UK and USA. It was already a strong tradition in public schools and universities, whereas the ordinary working man had to work six days a week. Working-class sportsmen found it hard to play top-level sport because they had to work. As professional teams developed, some clubs were willing to make 'broken time' payments to players, that is, to pay top sportsmen to take time off work. As attendances increased, it became possible to pay men to concentrate on their sport full time.

There were still many who believed money to be a terrible influence on sport, and upheld amateurism. Supporters of **professionalism** claim it is best for players to receive pay as an incentive additional to personal motivation. The middle and upper classes supported amateurism because this prevented the working classes from competing against them. Working-class sportsmen needed the money to replace lost wages. There was a clash between those who wanted sport for all, and those who felt this destroyed 'playing for the love of the game'. This clash carried on for more than 100 years. Some sports dealt with it relatively easily, such as golf, which decided in the late-1800s to allow competition between amateurs and professionals. Others were traumatised by the dilemma, and took generations to fully come to terms with professionalism.

Problems can arise for amateur sportsmen when sponsors offer to help them with playing expenses in the hope of striking lucrative endorsement deals with them in case they become professionals at a later date. The deals could jeopardise their status as amateurs and, if left unchecked, may be seen as corruption or cheating. Where professionals are permitted, it is hard for amateurs to compete against them.

Even the Olympic Games have had conflict with this issue. By the early twenty-first century, they had accepted professional sports people representing their countries – multi-millionaires from the tennis and soccer worlds, for example. The majority of athletes have to have sponsors to be able to train and finance the sort of equipment necessary in sports today. So we could ask is anyone truly amateur?

John (amateur sportsman): I would never compete for money.

Steve (professional sportsman): Well, I have a family to look after.

John: Well, I work, so I can compete for the love of my sport.

Steve: Being paid means I can get to the top of my sport because I have time to train.

John: I enjoy what I do…it's not an industry or occupation to me.

Steve: I will take whatever they pay me now. It will set me up for life. It may seem a lot of money, but injury could stop me at any time so I need to earn it now. Would you take sponsorship which still means you are amateur?

John: No, because it is payment by the back door. Doesn't really go with my ethics. Money has ruined sport in my opinion.

Tiger Woods – a professional golfer

Gary Wolstenholme – an amateur golfer

Task

Using the information and conversation on this page, explain the issues arising from the debate between professional and amateur sports people.

Now you know about money and sport

Issues involved in sport

Prejudice and **discrimination** are key issues in the sporting arena today. Over the last 30 years, there have been great strides made in trying to eradicate prejudice in sport. There have been well-known campaigns and high-profile cases to prevent prejudice from happening.

With regards to **racism**, there has been the 'Let's Kick Racism Out of Football' campaign. Black players now feel protected and, where abuse does occur, the clubs, the FA and FIFA have a duty to act. 2002 saw Slovakia abuse the England team; Spain 2004 saw Ashley Cole and Shaun Wright-Phillips abused, and 2008 saw black players targeted in Croatia. In all cases fines were levied.

In 2008, Sol Campbell was abused in a racist and homophobic way when he was playing for Portsmouth against Tottenham. Tottenham promised that anyone found guilty of this would be banned for life. The 2008 F1 season saw high-profile abuse of Lewis Hamilton in the Spanish Grand Prix. So, although it does happen, there is total condemnation of such actions.

Racism is not just about the chants of fans; it can happen between players too. In January 2008, a race row erupted over claims that the Indian cricketer Harbajan Singh racially abused Andrew Symonds by calling him a monkey. The International Cricket Council (ICC) then had to investigate these accusations.

All religions believe that any form of discrimination is wrong. It goes against teachings from holy books and present-day religious leaders. People are equal and should not be judged in a negative way. The teachings on pages 2–3 in the introductory section of this book will be useful here.

Disability

This was once a major issue in terms of access to sports facilities for disabled sports men and women. However, disability no longer precludes a person from sports. Not everybody in disability sport wants to, or indeed could, compete at the levels of those in the picture.

'There's more to it than that. Disability sport is about creating opportunities and making sport accessible to everyone, regardless of their ability. It's about enabling and encouraging disabled people to take part in sport simply for fun and enjoyment, whether that sport be tennis, sailing, horse riding, archery or scuba diving. With more than 50,000 members throughout the country, Disability Sport England helps make healthy lifestyle and participation in sport a reality for thousands of disabled people, be they aspiring junior basketball champions, Paralympic medal winners or simply people keen to take part in their chosen leisure pursuit.'

(Disability Sport England)

Now you know about some issues in sport

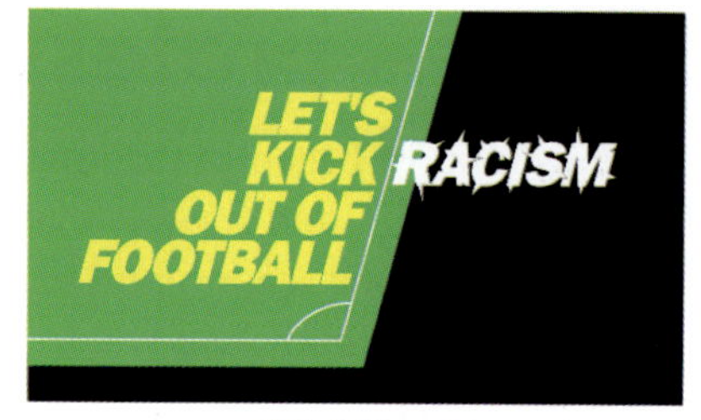

www.kickitout.org

Research Task

Racism has been an issue in many sports. Find out about one such incident and how it was dealt with. Do you think it solved the problem (in that instance, or in the long term)?

Task

In groups of three or four, research the issues in sport discussed on this page. Produce a news article looking at incidents of racism in sport and the disability issues. It should cover what has happened, what action has been taken and also how religious people have responded.

Britain's Paralympics team with medals, 2008

Exam tips

AO2 questions

These are evaluative questions, and each full question will include two of these – one worth 3 marks, the other worth 6 marks. You have to do well on these because they make up 50 per cent of the total mark. Let's check them out…

Evaluative questions always ask you what you think about something, or whether you agree. Actually, the exam isn't interested in whether or not you agree – it wants to know your reasoning. As long as you explain your reasons clearly, and you discuss the statement you were set, you should get marks.

3-mark AO2s

These start with a statement and then ask, 'What do you think? Explain your opinion.' The examiner is interested in your opinion as long as it relates to the statement. You will get marks for making a couple of points and then explaining them, perhaps with an example to strengthen your argument. The exam watchdog – QCA – wants to see opportunities for you to give personal insights, and this is where you do that. Let's try a couple…

1 **Religious people should do everything possible to win.** What do you think? Explain your opinion.

2 **Religious people should never play sports for money.** What do you think? Explain your opinion.

You can use general answers because religious people hold views that would be said to be secular answers, but you must include a religious comment because the statement refers to religious people.

Level	Criteria	Mark
0	Unsupported opinion or no relevant evaluation.	0
1	Opinion (e.g. I agree) supported by one simple reason.	1
2	Opinion supported by two simple reasons, or one elaborated reason.	2
3	Opinion supported by one well-developed reason, or a series of simple reasons, on one or both sides.	3

Getting used to the techniques of how to answer different types of questions effectively is really important. Quite often, good technique means you can answer more clearly and in a snappier style – this helps to make it easy for the examiner to give you better marks!

6-mark AO2s

OK, for these you've got to do a whole lot more work. For a start, you will have to have some religion in there – 3 marks max if you don't. Somewhere in the question there will be a prompt to remind you. Then, you have to answer from two sides, in other words you have to agree *and* disagree, each time explaining your ideas – 4 marks max if you don't.

So let's build from the 3-marker because the first levels for these questions are the same. Let's try a couple…

3 **A Holy Day should always be a day of rest.** Do you agree? Give reasons for your answer, showing you have thought about more than one point of view. Refer to religious arguments in your answer.

4 **Sport can never be called a religion.** Do you agree? Give reasons for your answer, showing you have thought about more than one point of view. Refer to religious arguments in your answer.

Level	Criteria	Mark
4	Opinion supported by two developed reasons, with reference to religion.	4
5	Evidence of reasoned consideration of two different points of view, with reference to religion.	5
6	A well-argued response, with evidence of reasoned consideration of two different points of view and clear reference to religion.	6

'Developed' means you said something and then explained it a bit.

'Reasoned consideration' just means 'some reasons with explanations'.

Topic Three Religion and work

In this topic you are going to be studying various aspects of **work**, business and **enterprise**. You will need to be aware of the religious teachings of at least one faith and learn to apply these to the issues raised throughout the topic. Work is an important aspect of most adults' lives and you will need to understand religious attitudes to the purpose and importance of work.

For many religious people, work is more than just a job; it is a **vocation**. Work is regarded as a service and a way of life. Work is not always paid or carried out for personal gain. Many religious people would say that work needs to be fulfilling and purposeful. You will need to know examples of individuals who have regarded work as a vocation. You will also need to understand the importance of **voluntary work** and be able to describe the work of at least one religious voluntary organisation.

In this topic, there are also moral issues connected with aspects of business and enterprise that you will need to discuss and understand. For example, is it acceptable to make money through any industry, or are some professions ethically wrong for religious people to be connected with? What are religious views of the economy and taxation? What standards should be expected from **employers** to ensure that **employees** are treated properly in the workplace?

All industries involve people and so you will be using teachings and beliefs to examine religious attitudes to employers and employees. Many issues can arise in the workplace for religious believers. For example, how should people be treated at work? Should employers make allowances for religious believers in order for them to practise their faith at work? What about the unemployed – who should be supporting those who, for whatever reason, may not be able to earn a living?

A good place to start is to think about your own attitudes to work.

Task

1 Make a list of the things you do that could be regarded as work? Why do you do these tasks? Who do you do them for? Do you gain anything from doing the tasks? Would it matter if you didn't do them? Discuss your ideas with the rest of the class.

Evaluate your opinions by completing the following phrases:

Work is…

It is important to work because…

I enjoy work when…

I don't enjoy work when…

The future

By now, you will have already started to think about the kind of work you want to do when you leave school. Most young people have ambitions to be successful – to have a career rather than just any old job that will pay the bills. One way that this can be achieved is to have some definite goals in mind.

Task

2 a If you had to say where you will be work-wise in ten years' time, what would you say?

b Make a list of the steps you need to take to get you to that point.

Now you have thought about work

Employers and employees

The government issues guidance, as well as laws, to govern business practices and the relationships between employers (companies and people who create jobs and pay people) and employees (anyone who works for a company or person in return for wages or a salary). In this section, you are going to look at some aspects of these relationships.

Find out more about employers' and employees' rights at: www.direct.gov.uk.

Minimum wage

• Workers aged 22 and over	£5.73 an hour
• Workers aged 18–21	£4.77 an hour
• Young people (those older than school leaving age and younger than 18)	£3.53 an hour

As of 2008

Minimum wage

In the UK, most employees over the age of 16 have a legal right to a minimum pay per hour for the work they do. This rate is set annually by the government and is called the **minimum wage**. This applies to all types of work. Companies must pay their employees at least this amount per hour, whether full or part time.

When the minimum wage was introduced in 1999, some people argued that it was not necessary and that it would force companies out of business. For over 2 million people, this meant an increase of up to a third in their wage packets. It showed that many people had been badly underpaid for the work they did, and that companies were making profits by exploiting their workers.

Others argued that people should be entitled to a fair day's pay for their work and that the low paid need protection from unethical employers. People on minimum wages are often living near the poverty line and the minimum wage is one way to ensure that families have at least enough money in the household to provide essential needs.

TUC

Research conflicts involving trade unions and the methods of **protest** and pressure used to gain employee rights such as strikes, picket lines and work to rule. Present your findings to the rest of the class.

Trade unions

The **United Nations' (UN)** Declaration of Human Rights (see page 78) applies to the world of work, including the right to form and join a trade union. A trade union is an organisation that represents the rights of employees within an industry. Their role is to ensure that employers provide their employees with fair working conditions, reasonable pay and working hours, and that the company meets health and safety requirements, etc.

Trade unions represent and advise employees of their rights. As they represent large numbers of people, they can negotiate pay increases, changes to contracts, provision of health and safety training, and so on. This is important because individual employees often can't take on their employer for fear of losing their job. However, tensions often arise between government, companies and trade unions, as each group seeks to protect what it feels is important.

Types of Industry

Primary industry – getting raw materials from the natural environment, e.g. mining, farming, fishing.

Secondary industry – manufacturing (making things), e.g. cars, textiles, furniture.

Tertiary industry – providing a service, e.g. teaching, social work, hospitality.

Quaternary industry – work involved in research and development, e.g. IT, science, pharmaceuticals.

Now you know about employers/employees

Religious attitudes to work

Buddhism

'Cease to do evil. Learn to do good.'
(The Dhammapada)

The bases of the teachings of the Buddha are the Four Noble Truths and the Noble Eightfold Path. For Buddhists today, the teachings provide the guidance they need to leave behind negative views and develop positive qualities that will help them on the path to enlightenment. Following the path fully includes the working life of a believer. Right livelihood is the fifth step of the path and relates to the work a Buddhist may do.

To be true to the principles of Buddhism, a believer should not earn a living through the suffering of others, for example, selling tobacco, weapons or meat. The work Buddhists do should

Christianity

'Faith without works is dead.' (St Paul)

Throughout the Bible, there are many references to the purpose and importance of work. In the creation story, Adam and Eve are cast out of the Garden of Eden and told they must work as a punishment for their sin. They are told that their food would be gained by the sweat of their brow: work is therefore necessary for human survival. This belief is also seen in the New Testament where Paul states that those who refuse to work will not eat. In doing so, Paul warns Christians against laziness and relying on others to support them.

Many Christians today would agree that work is more than just a way to make a living. Work enables people to be creative and use the talents

Hinduism

'A man doing his dharma leads his soul to liberation.' (Bhagavad Gita)

The four main aims in life for a Hindu include artha – gaining wealth by lawful means. Work in Hinduism is tied directly to people's religious duties or dharma. Traditional Hindu teachings set people into castes according to their birth. Each caste has specific jobs that might be expected to be performed to earn a living. Brahmins were the highest caste and had the role of priests. Kshatriyas had **responsibility** for leadership and protection of society. Vaishyas were traders and farmers. Shudras were the lowest caste and worked as servants and doing manual jobs.

Task

Complete the tasks on pages 35–37 for the religion(s) that you are studying:

have positive intentions and not be motivated by greed and the desire for material possessions and personal ambition. Caring professions, such as medicine, social work and teaching, are considered particularly suitable because they provide opportunities for a believer to develop compassion and show respect for others.

The seventh step of the path – right awareness – is also important at work. In the modern world, many people work in high-stress situations. Work can also be repetitive and dull for some people. Buddhism emphasises the need to control the mind and make the most of every situation. By thinking positively and working in harmony with those around them, a Buddhist not only improves their own lives, but contributes to the happiness of others.

and skills that God has given them. It is a way to find meaning and purpose in life, especially when someone's work is dedicated to the service of others or enriching the lives of other people. Work also brings people together and helps to develop strong community links and give people a sense of belonging and value.

Many Christians believe that work should be a vocation and that God calls people to the service of others. For example, working in caring professions, joining the priesthood or missionary work is particularly respected. Whatever work a Christian does, there should also be time for leisure in their lives. The Ten Commandments include a day of rest to ensure that people are able to make time for worship and family life.

In Hindu society today, professional and office work is still considered to be better than manual work. However, within urban India the previously strict rules about caste are no longer adhered to. It is possible for a farmer's son to be a banker or a Brahmin's daughter to train as an air stewardess, and so on. In rural India, however, the caste system is often still followed and people work within their caste.

In the past, the outcastes or untouchables were permitted only to do the dirtiest jobs that no one within the caste system would do. Today, India has abolished the laws that discriminated against these people and has used positive discrimination to reserve places in schools and public sector jobs to be filled by people from this previously despised group.

1 Explain why religious believers consider it right to work to earn a living?
2 Why would a religious believer not want to perform some jobs?

Islam

'No one eats better food than that which they have earned by their own labours.'
(Hadith)

Work is an important part of a Muslim's life. Men are expected to work to support their family and make their contribution to the community through zakah. Even imams usually have another occupation, unless they have retired, as it is expected that those with the skills to lead the community will provide their services for free. The work that Muslims do must be in line with the basic principles of the faith. This means that it must be honest labour and their income should not be made from dishonourable actions such as gambling, cheating, sexual promiscuity or trading in alcohol.

Muslims are encouraged to use their talents to support the community. Working in industries such

Judaism

'Teach your son a trade or you teach him to be a robber.' (Talmud)

In Judaism, work is seen as an important aspect of adult life. The creation story sets out the need for work to sustain human life and harvest the benefits of G-d's creation. Humankind is given responsibility to care for creation as due payment for G-d's gifts. In the Ten Commandments, Jews are told that they must work for six days and set aside the Shabbat for worship, family and rest. In some ultra Orthodox communities, this means that no work at all must be undertaken during Shabbat unless it is a matter of life and death.

Work is seen as a necessary part of fulfilling G-d's will, and providing for a dignified life and support

Sikhism

'All work is noble if performed in the right way.'
(Adi Granth)

Sikhism expects all followers to pray, work and give. Guru Nanak made it clear that work was a religious duty and dismissed the practices of some men during his time who devoted themselves to spiritual exercises and depended on the support of others to meet their essential needs. The Guru said that work was a way to honour and serve God, providing it was honestly done.

Today, Sikhs are free to work in any profession providing it does not conflict with their religious beliefs. Working in industries that are dishonest, exploit others or involve trading in alcohol or tobacco would conflict with Sikh teaching. The principle of kirat karna – honest work – applies. This means that any dignified work, whether

Task

3 Explain how work can help a believer in their spiritual development.
4 Make a list of jobs – label each 'recommended' (i.e. positively following the teachings of that religion); 'accepted' (i.e. would be allowed by the religion); or 'forbidden' (i.e. not appropriate for a follower of that religion). Then explain each label.
5 **It is not important to have a career if you are religious**. What do you think? Explain your opinion.

as medicine, education, social welfare, science and technology are particularly valued because the work is beneficial to others. These professions are called *fard kifiyah* (collective duties) because it is the responsibility of the community to ensure that these essential jobs are filled with people who have the skills to meet society's needs. This is to ensure that the needs of those vulnerable in society are met. For example, children, the sick, the elderly and disabled.

When Muslims make the Hajj to Makkah, all wear white to emphasise that everyone is equal. This attitude is reflected in Prophet Muhammad's (pbuh) teaching about work. He emphasised that no one should see themselves as superior because of the work they do or the pay they receive. All wealth belongs to Allah and everyone who works honestly to support the community is valuable. People who work in manual trades, for example, are just as necessary to society as company directors.

of one's family. In the past, this would have been the main responsibility of the man, but in modern times, Jewish women have taken on equal responsibility in fulfilling this role. Jews can undertake any profession or job providing that it does not go against the general teaching and principles of the faith. Work that is dishonest or degrading, such as illegal trading or pornography, should be avoided.

Jewish teaching also includes advice on how to conduct business and fair trade. The Torah makes clear that traders must be honest and that consumers can expect recompense if they are wrongly sold something. There is also an expectation of fair competition between tradesman and the teachings emphasise that it is wrong for someone to try to force another business to close by unfair means.

manual or professional, can be performed by Sikhs. Work that is socially useful is considered particularly important as it can help someone develop the qualities to become nearer to mukti – understanding of the true self and release from rebirth.

An important aspect of the Sikh work ethic is the performing of sewa – selfless service. This is a form of voluntary work performed in the gurdwara and the local community. All Sikhs are encouraged to contribute their services for the good of all, as well as a means of being spiritually uplifted. This work might be helping with the langar – cooking, serving food and cleaning – or it could be in the community working with the elderly or community groups. The Guru Granth Sahib makes it clear that such selfless service will enable someone to achieve liberation.

6 **How much you earn is not important if you are enjoying your job**. Do you agree? Give reasons for your answer, showing you have thought about more than one point of view. Refer to religious arguments in your answer.

Now you know about religious attitudes to work

Work as a vocation

For the exam, you will need to understand the term 'vocation' and be able to write about at least one case study of a religious person who has regarded work as a vocation. This can be a well-known individual or a case study based on a profession that especially employs religious people.

For many people, work is more than just a way to make a living. Some people feel that they have been called to work in a particular profession. Whilst there may be material gain, such as a good career, respect and good pay, people who describe their work as a vocation would say that these are not the main reasons why they work where they do. Work as a vocation is usually linked with service to others. Doctors and nurses, teachers, priests and those doing voluntary work overseas often see their work as a vocation.

Religious people may describe their work as a calling directly from God. They believe that God wants them to fulfil a special task, regardless of what it might require them to give up or the danger they may find themselves in. Throughout history, there have been many people who have regarded work in this way. The Bible records several examples including the stories of Jonah and the whale and the calling of the disciples.

I teach in an inner-city school because I believe that education can help young people to improve their lives.

A teacher

I became a doctor because I want to help people. In my work, I meet all kinds of people and I treat everyone with dignity and respect.

A doctor

A war correspondent

I have a vocation to tell the truth about what is happening around the world.

A priest

God called me to carry out his mission on earth. My work includes providing pastoral support for all who live within the diocese.

Vocation – a calling to work in a specific field; called by God for special work.

The Basics

1. What is meant by work as a vocation?
2. How is a vocation different to other kinds of work?
3. Read the speech bubbles of people working in professions that might be regarded as vocations. For each one, explain why their work is more than just a job.
4. Describe the work of one religious believer who has regarded work as a vocation.
5. **Religious believers should also work in industries that help other people.** What do you think? Explain your opinion.

Now you have thought about work as a vocation

Mother Teresa

'My God out of love for you, I desire to remain and do whatever be your holy will.' (Mother Teresa)

Agnes Bojaxhiu was born in Albania in 1910 and raised as a Roman Catholic. She was always fascinated by stories about the lives of missionaries and their service to others. By the age of 12, Agnes was determined that she must commit herself to a religious life. At the age of 18, she left home to join the Sisters of Loreto and would never see her family again.

In 1929, Agnes arrived in India where she took her vows as a nun and adopted the name Teresa after the patron saint of missionaries. At first, the young nun worked in a school in Calcutta teaching children. However, she became more and more troubled by the terrible poverty she saw and, in particular, the lack of dignity and compassion shown for those who were literally dying in the streets.

In September 1946, Mother Teresa described her experience of 'the call within the call' and resolved to leave the security of a convent and live among the poor. She adopted a simple white sari with a blue border and began her missionary work tending to the homeless, starving and dying. Her first year was a testing experience; she had no income and had to beg for food and supplies, but her faith in God's will for her kept her going.

Over the next few years, she established the Missionaries of Charity. Its mission was to care for the hungry, the crippled, the blind, the lepers and all those who were uncared for by society and shunned by everyone. In 1952, Mother Teresa opened the first free hospice for the poor. Its purpose was to provide the dying with a dignified and beautiful death. Those brought to the hospice received medical attention and the last rites according to their faith.

By the time of her death in 1997, Mother Teresa had achieved worldwide recognition. She has been given many honours, including the Nobel Peace Prize. Her work has branched out into over 610 missions in 123 countries of the world. These missions include hospices for those with AIDS, leprosy and TB, soup kitchens for the poor and homeless, orphanages and schools. In 2003, the Pope bestowed the title 'Blessed' upon her, and many feel it will not be long before she is revered as a saint.

Think about the following:

Is 'vocation', our conscience, or God, or something else?
Does society do better or worse by having people who feel a vocation?
Is 'vocation' always religious?

That 1946 moment

Teresa was on a train on her way to a new posting. She said that she suddenly knew she had to go back to Calcutta but not as a teacher. God was telling her that she had to go back, to work with the sick, orphaned and dying. That moment changed her life and the lives of many others.

The Basics

Find out more about the life and work of Mother Teresa. Present your findings as a biography.

Now you know about work as a vocation

Voluntary work

It is easy to think of work as simply something that people do primarily for themselves to make money. However, every day, millions of people around the world are involved in work that is unpaid. They do not have to do this; it is something they choose to do for the benefit of others. Work of this kind is called voluntary work.

Voluntary work can take many different forms and people have many reasons for why they might choose to do voluntary work. For some people, this may simply involve a couple of hours of their time now and then collecting money for charity; for others, it can be a lifetime of service. For religious people, voluntary work is a way that they can put their faith into action. For example, in the Parable of the Sheep and Goats, Christians learn about the importance of serving others. For Sikhs, sewa (service to others) is an important religious duty and a form of worship.

The Basics

1. What is voluntary work?
2. Describe three different examples of work that might be done by a volunteer.
3. Explain three reasons why voluntary work is important to charities.
4. Explain why a religious believer might want to be involved in doing voluntary work. Refer to beliefs and teachings in your answer.

What the volunteers say

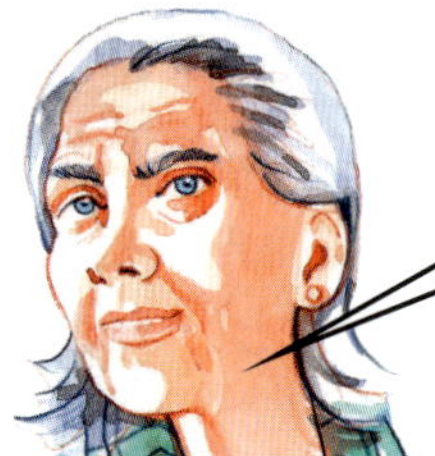

When I retired I felt I still had a lot to give, so I now do a few hours a week to help keep the shop open every day.

A charity shop

The staff here were so supportive when my husband was dying; the least I can do is help out.

Friends of the Hospital

I am a qualified engineer and when I heard about the devastation caused by the civil war, I wanted to do more than just give a few pounds.

Voluntary Service Overseas

Many of the people I meet here don't have family who can visit and talk to them. I think it helps them to cope seeing a friendly face every week.

Prison visitor

I was in the scouts myself; I love organising activities for the youngsters and it gives them something to be involved in where they can make friends and learn new skills.

Scout leader

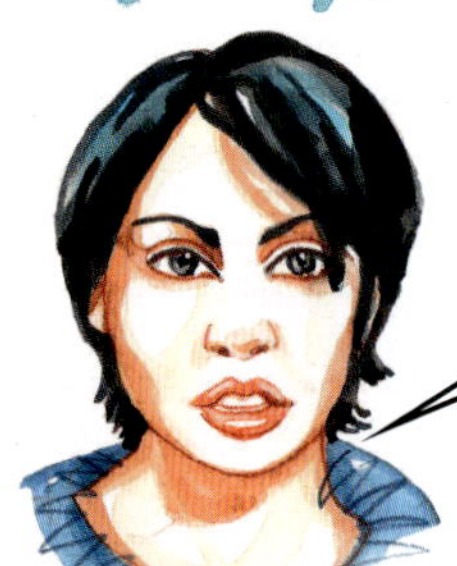

I have always enjoyed working with animals, and people often don't realise the charity couldn't continue without volunteers.

Animal sanctuary

Now you know about voluntary work

The Salvation Army and Street Pastors

The Salvation Army – organisation profile

The Salvation Army was set up by William Booth in the nineteenth century. Its mission statement is to proclaim the Gospel, persuade people of all ages to become practising Christians, and to be involved in a programme of practical concern for the needs of humanity. Jesus' message was one of love – God is love – and the Army tries to mirror this in its work. The Bible also emphasises that faith without good deeds is useless. The belief in agape – Christian love – is central to the work of The Salvation Army. The members of the organisation come into regular contact with many needy people, and so it is ideally placed to offer help and support.

The Salvation Army's first shelter to feed the hungry and provide beds for the homeless was set up in 1887 by Booth's son, at his request. Today, there is a nationwide network of homes, hostels and support centres. These provide for the needs of the homeless, unemployed and destitute. The Army regularly comes into contact with people who are addicted to drugs and alcohol. As part of its beliefs, all members of the Army commit to a lifestyle without alcohol because they see at first hand the damage that it can do to individuals and their families. The Army also runs soup kitchens and has a team of outreach workers in London who specifically work on getting the homeless back into permanent accommodation.

Find out more about the work of the Salvation Army at: www.salvationarmy.org.uk.

Street Pastors – organisation profile

In 2003, the Ascension Trust launched a new initiative to deal with the many problems facing young people living in urban areas. The Street Pastors are made up of volunteers from many different church backgrounds who are especially concerned for young people who feel marginalised from society and are vulnerable to falling into lifestyles of crime and drug abuse. There are now street pastors to be found in over 120 locations in the UK and the organisation has just begun to spread overseas.

The Street Pastor works in their community by going out into the streets and meeting young people in their own environment. Their ministry is often carried out at night, in sometimes dangerous and run-down areas of the cities. Their aim is to earn the respect and credibility of young people by listening to their needs and concerns and helping in an unconditional way. They want to show that the Church is there for them in a practical way, and ensure that every young person they meet will know there is someone there for them if they need them.

Find out more about the work of Street Pastors at: www.streetpastors.co.uk.

The Basics

1 Describe the work of one voluntary organisation.
2 **People who do voluntary work for large organisations that raise funds should be paid.** Do you agree? Give reasons for your answer, showing you have thought about more than one point of view. Refer to religious teachings in your answer.

Unemployment

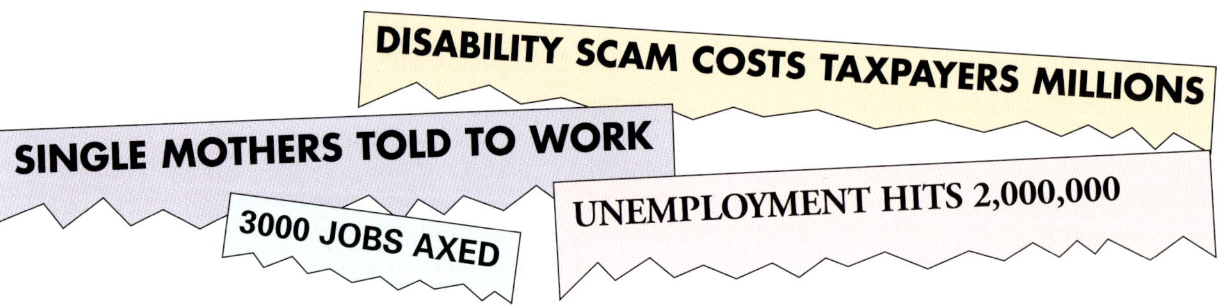

Unemployment is the term used to describe adults who, for whatever reason, are without a job and have no regular earnings. Many people experience unemployment at some time in their lives. Fortunately for most people living in the UK, it is a temporary situation brought about by personal circumstances, such as changing jobs or taking a career break to raise a family. People in these circumstances are often not counted in unemployment figures because they are unlikely to claim benefits.

For some people, unemployment can lead to desperate circumstances. Having no wages coming into the home each week can lead many families into living in relative poverty. It is easy for some people to say that 'It's their own fault' and, yes, there probably are people out there who are unemployed because they are not motivated to get a job. However, the reality of unemployment is that it is not always that simple and, for many people, the psychological impact of being without work is as bad as the financial impact.

One reason why there will always be some people who are unemployed is simply the way the economy works. Paying employees is one of the largest expenses a company has to make, so when a business is struggling and costs need to be cut, losing employees is one way to achieve this. There are also factors such as changes in the economy – the skills that employers need are constantly developing. This can particularly affect older people who lose their jobs. If they have been working in the same industry for 30 years, they may not have the skills needed in the new economic climate.

Unemployment doesn't only affect the individual; it can also affect whole communities. Throughout the UK, there are many examples of places that have become run down as a consequence of the large-scale loss of jobs in an area. If a large company in a town closes down or moves location, hundreds of local people can be left without work. This means that the locals no longer have the money to spend in their community. Other smaller businesses and industries in the area may well be forced to close too, when their customer base is reduced.

Causes of unemployment

- Lack of education or skills.
- Redundancy.
- Changes in the economy.
- Wages below social security benefits.
- Laziness.
- Automation replacing workers.
- Disability or illness.
- Age.
- Seasonal changes.
- Personal choice.

Discuss these causes of unemployment.
Society helps these people through the benefits system.
Are there any reasons which make you think society should help more? Why?
Are there any reasons which make you think society should not help? Why?

The possible effects of unemployment

- Low self-esteem.
- Unable to pay bills.
- Family break-up.
- Stress and ill health.
- Drug abuse (especially alcohol).
- Changed lifestyle.
- Homelessness.
- Rising crime figures.
- Run-down communities.
- Suicide.

Discuss these effects. Can you add any more? Split them into three groups: effects on the individual; family; and the community.

What can be done about unemployment?

Most unemployed people need financial support. This is done through taxation. Workers pay taxes and some of this money is used to give an income to the unemployed through social security benefits. Unemployment benefit is well below what would be considered an average living wage, and many of the long-term unemployed live in relative poverty.

Different government departments set up initiatives to enable people to learn new skills that are useful in a changing workplace. When an area has been affected by high unemployment, government grants and programmes are used to stimulate new industry and development to create jobs.

The community

Most communities have councils, private businesses and charitable organisations that also provide support for the unemployed. They may provide for immediate needs like food, clothing and shelter for the homeless. However, they may also provide things like free leisure facilities and training opportunities to encourage people to stay active and positive while they are looking for new work.

Religious traditions encourage believers to work to earn a living; idleness is frowned upon. However, they also teach respect and understanding and that when someone is in need they should be supported. Helping the poor and giving to charitable causes is a religious duty within all faiths. Religious teachings make clear that all people are equal in dignity and should be treated with respect and compassion. Religious congregations support the unemployed in practical ways, as well as spiritually through prayer and fellowship.

The Basics

1. Explain three reasons why someone may be unemployed.
2. Describe the possible effects of long-term unemployment.
3. Explain why the government gives benefits to the unemployed.
4. Explain the attitude of religious believers to unemployment.
5. **The unemployed should have to do voluntary work to earn their social security benefits.** Do you agree? Give reasons for your answer, showing you have thought about more than one point of view. Refer to religious arguments in your answer.

Now you know about unemployment

The economy

The economy is all the business and enterprise activities that take place within society. Most companies operate fairly and within government guidelines. Employers are free to pay employees what they consider to be fair wages that are at least the minimum wage. Many people in professions earn considerably more than this and may also have other benefits, such as a company car, free health care, a bonus and longer holidays.

Employers and employees sign a contract that will state the expectations of both sides. The contract is like a promise made between the two parties. The employer will promise to provide training, a salary, healthy working conditions, compassionate leave, and so on. The employee will promise to work specified hours, follow the code of conduct within the company, complete certain tasks, etc. If either party breaks the contract, there are legal routes to protect everyone's interests.

An important part of the economy is the government raising money through taxation to run the country. The armed forces and services, such as health, education and the police force, are all paid for by the government from taxation. Individuals pay taxes from their earnings in direct taxation (a percentage taken from their wages) and indirect taxation (the taxes paid whenever anything is bought – few products are tax free!) Companies also pay taxes to the government in a similar way.

It has been said that 'there is nothing as certain as death and taxes'. What do you think this means? Why do you think people always complain about paying taxes?
Do you think they would complain more if there were no police officers, teachers, nurses or fire services? How could these services be paid for if not by tax? Would that be better? Why?

Buddhism

'Better to swallow a ball of iron, than to lead a wicked and unrestrained life.'
(The Dhammapada)

Christianity

'Through work humanity not only transforms nature but it also achieves fulfilment.'
(Pope John Paul II)

Hinduism

'Doing the work of your dharma for work is better than idleness.'
(Bhagavad Gita)

Islam

'He who brings goods for sale is blessed, but he who keeps them till the price rises is cursed.'
(Hadith)

Judaism

'Do not weary yourself to become rich.'
(Proverbs)

Sikhism

'He who gathers wealth by oppressing others is cursed.'
(Guru Granth Sahib)

The Basics

1 Explain the terms:
   a employer
   b employee
   c minimum wage
   d trade union
   e employment contract
   f taxation.
2 Why would many religious believers agree with having a minimum wage?
3 **A religious person should not belong to a trade union.** What do you think? Explain your opinion.

Now you know about the economy

A religious perspective

All religious traditions regard work as important. For many religious people, work is an important part of practising their faith in everyday life. People from all different faiths can be found working in all sectors of the employment structure. However, some professions may not attract members of certain faiths because they would consider the work to be in conflict with their religious beliefs. For example, you would be unlikely to find a Buddhist working as a butcher or a Sikh employed in a distillery.

For religious people, part of earning is also being able to contribute financially to the upkeep of their local community. Churches, synagogues, and so on, are funded by the congregation. Many people pay a regular sum of money as a tithe to their religious community. This can be used for the upkeep of the holy building, to pay the religious leader and for various charitable causes. In addition to meeting the religious requirements, such as zakah in Islam or giving alms in Buddhism, many religious people also give gifts of money and their time to many worthwhile causes.

Today, work can often be a consuming and formidable strain on the individual. The increase in technology and the pace of the global economy has made little provision for the ideals found in many religious teachings. For example, the relaxation of the Sunday trading laws in the UK has meant that many people find themselves working seven days a week. Employers are not always sympathetic to the religious convictions of their employees. In the UK, many national holidays happen to coincide with Christian festivals, but this is not always the case for people of other faiths who may be forced to use up their holiday time or take unpaid leave in order to fulfil their religious obligations.

Buddhism 

'This is the highest blessing; generosity and good conduct.'
(The Dhammapada)

Christianity 

'Sell everything you have and give to the poor and you will have riches in heaven.'
(Jesus)

Hinduism

'Happiness arises from contentment, the pursuit of wealth will result in unhappiness.'
(Laws of Manu)

Islam 

'Those who seek riches out of greed are like people who eat but are never full.'
(Hadith)

Judaism 

'Do not do wrong in measuring land or weight or liquid.'
(Leviticus)

Sikhism

'A place in God's court can only be achieved if we do service for others.'
(Guru Granth Sahib)

The Basics

1. Explain, using beliefs and teachings, how a religious believer should use their earnings.
2. Explain how an employer with religious beliefs should treat their employees.
3. **It does not matter what work you do if the job is well paid.** Do you agree? Give reasons for your answer, showing you have thought about more than one point of view. Refer to religious teachings in your answer.

Now you know about religious perspectives

Exam practice

All questions in the exam are written to test your ability to respond to the assessment objectives (AO1 and AO2). You have already looked at tips for AO2 in Sport and Leisure, Topic Two (page 31). Let's take a look at AO1.

AO1 questions

In AO1 questions, you are being asked to show your knowledge and understanding of the topics. The questions will ask you to describe, explain and analyse the information you have learnt.

The AO1 questions will add up to a total of 9 marks. They can be broken up into a range of different mark allocations. There will be short answer questions of just 1, 2 and 3 marks that can be answered in a single word, phrase or short paragraph. Some questions will be worth 4, 5 or 6 marks and will need you to write longer answers, with more depth and explanation.

You can spot when you need to say more about any point you make by the question language. If it says 'Explain ...' you always have to say a bit more about each point you make, either by explanation or example. Similarly, 'Describe ...' needs more about each point – again either by explanation or example.

The 9 marks will be split up in different ways. The questions might be worth 1, 2 and 6 marks or 3 and 6 marks or 2, 2 and 5 marks. They will always include a mix of short and longer answers.

Make up some exam questions of your own for AO1. Remember, they must total 9 marks.

Sample 1-mark questions

1 What is meant by the term 'tithe'?

2 What is meant by the term 'minimum wage'?

Sample 2-mark questions

3 Give two reasons why people work?

4 Explain briefly what is meant by taxation.

Sample 3-mark questions

5 Describe the work of one individual who has regarded work as a vocation.

6 Give three reasons why some religious believers do voluntary work.

Sample 4-mark questions

7 Explain why some religious believers experience problems keeping religious duties while they are working.

8 Describe the work of one voluntary organisation.

Sample 5-mark questions

9 Explain why religious people might not want to work in some industries.

10 Explain why religious employers would want to ensure their employees are treated fairly.

Sample 6-mark questions

11 Explain how some religious believers would use part of their earnings to support others.

12 Explain, using beliefs and teachings, religious attitudes to work.

Remember, there will also be AO2 questions on this topic. Here's a couple for you to have a go at:

13 Religious people should not have jobs that involve killing. What do you think? Explain your opinion. (*3 marks*)

14 Having a successful career is more important than following a religion. Do you agree? Give reasons for your answer, showing you have thought about more than one point of view. Refer to religious arguments in your answer. (*6 marks*)

Topic Four Religion and multicultural society

In this topic you will be looking at the diverse nature of British society today. Since the end of the First World War, much has changed. Britain has moved from a mainly 'white' population to a mixture of races all over the country. People came to work here, often doing the jobs British people didn't want to do after the war or where there weren't enough workers. Today, we have **refugees** arriving as they believe they will be safer here than in their own country. This could be the result of political change or war in their own countries. With the influx of people, we now have a greater range of religions, festivals, food, dress, buildings, languages and, as a result, things have had to change in the way that society is run.

So what is 'being British' today? Firstly, we live in a democratic country and this hasn't changed. We have a reigning monarch to represent us around the world; we have a choice of political parties to run our country and a right to change this every five years if we aren't satisfied. Religion is at the forefront of our society, and faith gives us our values. Church and State have always been closely linked, but should they be in the modern world? Times are changing – for better or for worse – and this is an issue to be discussed.

As people change, laws have to change to ensure that people are protected, but have some laws gone too far? Should Britain be open to all-comers? Are they a benefit or a problem? Do they hinder or do they enrich us as a nation?

Obviously, if you try to mix all these people together it is not going to be easy and history has shown this. Britain is a multicultural society, it is a moving society with **immigration** and **emigration**. Some areas of Britain now have a higher percentage of foreign nationals than indigenous people. Is this a good or bad thing or both?

Religion has changed as well. Fewer people than ever are attending church, yet religion seems to be a very important part of the lives of the various communities in Britain. These are all issues that this module of work will look at.

Has Britain gone too far to try to accommodate others, or not far enough?

Task

1 a Find out what the terms 'tolerance', 'respect' and 'diversity' mean.
  b Using examples, show how they are important to the changing society in Britain today.

Political correctness

As society has changed, Britain has had to move with the times. This is to protect the rights of individuals. To be **politically correct**, 'PC' as it is known, is now an expected attitude from all of us.

Task

2 'PC' is a term applied to language, ideas, policies or behaviour seen to minimise offence to gender, racial, cultural, disabled, aged or other identified groups. Any action/statement that can cause offence is unacceptable by law. Explain what you think about the following actual examples.
  a Would a Christmas card in a shop window offend non-Christians?
  b Would a person wearing full Muslim purdah offend non-Muslims?
  c Would the presence of a drug dog at an airport offend Muslim passengers?
  d Would a person wearing a cross and chain offend others?

When religion and politics clash

Politics is the process by which groups of people make decisions. The term is generally applied to the behaviour within civil governments – the running of the internal and external affairs of a country. Religion and politics have to deal with two spheres of activities in the life of the same person. **Citizens** who belong to a religious faith are also members of the secular society. It is often impossible to separate the two. People get morals from religions and these are seen in the way people express themselves in a secular society. If you like, you could think about it as two codes of conduct to live by. Fairness, justice, equality, democracy, respect for rules and each other are all principles that could be advocated by politicians or religious people.

Throughout history, there has been a conflict between politics and religion or between Church and State. On a leadership level, there was the quest to be the most powerful or influential amongst the people – the King v. the Pope, the King v. the Archbishop. Over the years, Britain has seen conflict amongst key figures. Henry VIII and Archbishop Cranmer, or the battle between the Catholics and the Protestants in Ireland in recent times, for example. There is the clash with Islam and politics both in Western countries and in Muslim State countries. We have to remember that in Islamic countries, the religion is the politics. In France, the ruling government put a ban on people wearing religious objects because France is run on secular principles.

On an individual level, there are decisions to be made about contemporary issues – marriage, divorce, sex, contraception, suicide, abortion, euthanasia, war, food laws, clothing, lifestyles and terrorism. Often, the decisions are affected by religious beliefs. When the law conflicts with what people believe God is telling them, decisions can be very difficult to make.

Religious leaders do sometimes criticise political decisions and their views can be influential

Task

Read the situations below. What is the conflict in each one and what should be the solution?

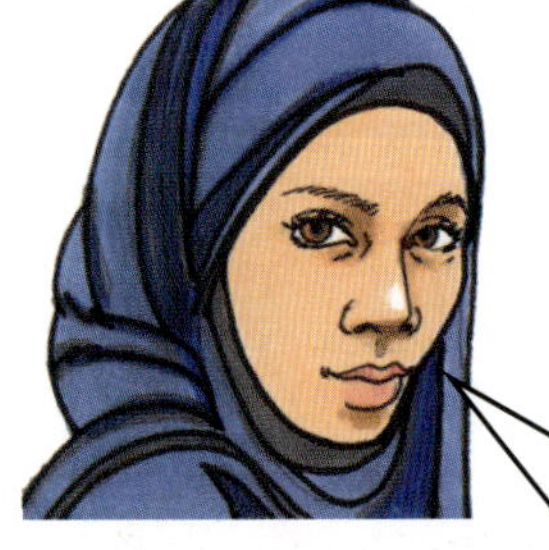

Do political and religious laws mix?

The Ten Commandments given to Moses have actually formed the basis of the laws of many nations. So, these religious laws have, in fact, become political laws.

Buddhism 

'A man should hasten towards the good . . . restrain thoughts from evil.' (Dhammapada)

Buddhism has guidelines on how to live in order to achieve good karma and, ultimately, nirvana. Laws are a positive, upholding force in society, not just a restrictive power. Good rulers uphold just laws. State laws can represent the values of the religion, for example. They can help to maintain the value of non-harming by prohibiting murder, or the value of not taking what is not freely given by punishing theft.

Christianity 

St Paul said that a ruler of the land is put there by God so should be obeyed. If the State is corrupt, Christians may feel that they should challenge it, as in South America with the Liberation Theology movement. Within Britain, Church leaders sit in the House of Lords, so are part of the law-making system of this country. Laws do not always match up to ideals within Christianity. For example, divorce is legal, but this would not be recognised by the Catholic Church.

Hinduism

In the Laws of Manu, it states that 'Whoever hates the ruler will soon be destroyed'. Hindu law is always concerned with relative justice in any given situation, rather than having rigid rules that could lead to injustice. We see many instances with British law where justice is not done. It does lead us to believe that many State laws fail to achieve real justice in many circumstances. It is also very difficult to distinguish between sin and crime. Are they not part of the same thing? If you break a State law, then you are likely to have broken religious laws too, but bad karma is the result of both. When people fail to abide by the law, rulers (i.e. the State) have the divine prerogative to punish.

Islam 

The only true law according to Islam is Shari'ah law and, until this is instituted in all societies, there is no real justice. Shari'ah law is Qur'an based. However, Muslims are required to be good citizens which requires following British law. If they believe that this law is corrupt, then they feel that they have a duty to try to change it using peaceful means. Quite often there is conflict between the two ideals.

Judaism 

Jews believe that laws exist to keep society stable and protect individuals from exploitation. They focus on people's responsibilities not rights. Torah law is one that can punish but also encourage respect. Shabbat prayer in the synagogue prays for the State and government here, as well as the State of Israel. The monarchy is blessed, as G-d gave them authority so they should be obeyed. Jews respect the politics of the country they live in.

Sikhism 

Guru Tegh Bahadur said, 'Sikhs must always keep the law if it agrees with Sikh principles. If unjust…fight!' They, therefore, keep the State laws where they live. Good laws ensure harmonious management of human affairs. Justice is the key principle with the weakest in society protected. Sikhs have always lived under laws imposed by non-Sikhs.

Think about the question… do politics and religious laws clash?

Now you have thought about politics and religion

Church and State

Henry VIII broke away from the Catholic Church of Rome and established the Church of England in 1534 with The Act of Supremacy. Since then, politics and religion have been hard to separate. The ruling monarch is both the Head of State and the Head of the Church of England. The current monarch is represented by the prime minister as the elected leader of the country on a political level and the Archbishop of Canterbury as the Head of the Church on a religious level. As a constitutional monarch, the Queen does not 'rule' the country, but fulfils important ceremonial and formal roles with respect to the parliament of the United Kingdom, and the devolved assemblies of Scotland, Wales and Northern Ireland. Her title of 'Defender of the Faith' makes her the Head of the Church, but also respects the rights of people to their own faiths. So, clearly, politics and religion are connected – the Queen being the common thread.

Blasphemy laws

These were passed in 1838 when the Church was at the heart of society and therefore to challenge it or offend it was seen as criticising the whole fabric of society. However, in January 2008, the Liberal Democrat Evan Harris proposed that the offences of blasphemy and blasphemous libel, which made it illegal to insult Christianity, be scrapped. Harris had said that in multicultural Britain, 'given that these laws protect only the tenets of the Christian churches, they would appear to be plainly discriminatory.' The law now has an offence concerning 'inciting religious hatred', which covers all discrimination or offence against religion. MPs voted to support the abolition of blasphemy in an amendment to the Criminal Justice and Immigration Bill.

In groups, think about the following ideas. Share the feedback with the class.

- Should the law deal with what is essentially a religious matter, namely offending God?
- Should people be allowed to criticise religion? Is there a difference between criticising and making fun of religion?
- Does criticism automatically make something offensive?
- Does allowing someone to question and criticise make a religion stronger/faith deeper?
- In some countries, blasphemy is punished by the death penalty. What do you think about this?
- Are British laws better now that they cover offensive material against all religions?

Research Task

Islam is very strict about blasphemy laws. Research:

- the Salman Rushdie *Satanic Verses* incident
- the cartoons about the prophet Muhammad (pbuh) in Denmark
- the prophet Muhammad (pbuh) teddy bear incident in Sudan.

What do these tell us about the strength of feeling on this issue?

Freedom of choice

In Britain, we live in a political and religious democracy where each individual has the freedom of choice to vote, to decide who to vote for, to be a member of a faith or none at all, or to change from one faith to another. You don't have to complete any forms or register, or indeed face any punishment for the position you hold. (In Iran, for example, there is the death penalty if anyone converts from Islam to another faith. In Malaysia, you have to register your chosen religion with the government and again if you change it.) However, with this system, we all do have to respect the choices others make whether or not we agree with them.

*What do you think? Is it better to give people freedom of choice or no choice at all? Choice creates **diversity**. Does this cause a problem?*

Now you know about religion and law

Multicultural Britain

The phrase 'multicultural Britain' is one we hear often. In the modern world, people travel, move abroad, live in other countries – so we end up with a mixture of cultures. The term itself means that we recognise the rights of others to have their own beliefs, religion, language and culture and to be allowed to practise these in Britain today. However, it can seem as though there is no common thread, nothing to unite us all together.

What does this picture tell you about Britain today?

A Mori poll in 2008 found that 62 per cent of people believed that Britain was better because of being multicultural.

Why do you think this is the case?

However, 32 per cent felt it threatened the 'British way of life' and 54 per cent of people argued that 'areas of Britain, because of immigration don't feel like Britain anymore'.

Why do people hold these opinions?

What we have in Britain is separate communities living side by side rather than full integration. If people move here, they are more likely to move to an area where their own culture is already up and running – 'so they feel at home'. What really should happen is that people feel that they can live anywhere and live in peace, cooperation with and understanding of each other's diversity. In order for true **multiculturalism** to work, we need to understand and implement the 'key concepts' of **tolerance**, respect and diversity, along with the modern term, political correctness. All of these are qualities that religions would promote as well. So, with these ideas we are seeing the link between religion and political ideals.

Fashions

Food

Different cultures

Languages

Festivals

Knowledge

Religions

What does multiculturalism give us?

Task

1 As a class, organise a survey just for your class. Produce a graph to show the results. Use the following questions in your survey:
   - a Do you like living in Britain as it is today? Yes/No.
   - b Do you like living in a society with other cultures? Yes/No.
   - c What is the biggest impact area for you – growth in religious buildings, different foods available or the way people dress?
   - d If you went to a different country, would you prefer to live in an area with other British people? Yes/No.
   - e Does the presence of other cultures enrich our own? Yes/No/Don't know.

2 What summary would you make using the statistics from your graph?

The Basics

1 What does multicultural mean?

2 **Britain is a place where different people live in separate groups/cultures. This is not multiculturalism.** What do you think? Explain your opinion.

3 Using two of the key concepts, how would they lead to a better society?

Pros and cons of multicultural Britain

Read the following three speech bubbles:

Hi, I'm Alice, 21 years old and have just finished Uni in Manchester. This is a really diverse city – people of all races, religious backgrounds and cultures. I've learnt so much from other people and had loads of different experiences. I understand what people believe and why they do the things they do. I've visited a mosque and a Hindu temple, something at one time I could only have done abroad. Loads of fab food too on the Curry Mile! I saw the celebration of Chinese New Year in the China Town part of the city – firecrackers galore! Superb! Also, we've had loads of music gigs – all with a diverse audience. I have also noticed that actually we are not all that different after all. We have more in common than people like to admit. It must be quite hard to settle in a new country, so people do attach themselves to others from their culture. Whether it is true multiculturalism I'm not sure, but my experience of different people has definitely made my life more interesting.

Hello, I'm Jack, 50 years old and a builder by trade. I don't agree with this multiculturalism stuff. Too many differences between people cause problems – we cannot possibly understand everything and because people are different we tend to be scared or wary of them. If we look at society, there are just groups of people living in clusters – it's the odd person who really mixes. Society is more segregated than integrated. I feel people go for what they are used to and some communities have set themselves up to reflect the places they came from. Places have been nicknamed 'Little India', for example. Our way of life in Britain is changing and other cultures are becoming more prevalent whilst British culture is disappearing. If it could work, then good, but I don't think some people really want it to.

My name is Joel. I arrived from Jamaica with my family ten years ago. My children are both teenagers now. I suppose I see it from the other side. We came here for a better life – more work opportunities than back home, and a better future for our family. We live in London, which now has a large black community. We chose London as we felt more at home. It's hard being the 'different one', the one who stands out, and people do target you. It's also hard to forget your culture and, with greater numbers of immigrants, it is bound to influence Britain. Multiculturalism is hard to achieve and, though it is the ideal, I question whether it is possible.

Task

1 Read the views above about multiculturalism in Britain. Divide your page into advantages and disadvantages. List ideas on either side and add your own to the list.

2 In pairs, write a newspaper article on the issue of 'Multicultural Britain Today'. Use your experiences, what you have read or seen, your research carried out on the topic, or even the results of your survey. Remember, your writing has to be appropriate and supported by evidence. There must be a religious comment in your article. Use ICT, if available, to produce your article. *The idea of this is to explore the topic from many angles. This will mean that in the exam you will be able to answer any type of question set: what the term means, how it is implemented in British society, pros and cons. Remember, whilst many of the questions are different the actual material you need in your answers is the same – just applied differently.*

The UK – a moving society?

In Britain, we have an ever-changing population. The rest of the world is easy to access. Hence, there are people who want to emigrate and set up in another country. Statistics show a balance between immigration and emigration. Eastern Europe has seen many changes; Africa is very unstable through war; and the Middle East is unpredictable as religious fanaticism becomes more prevalent. Therefore, Britain, as well as other countries, is thought of by many as a safe haven.

There has been much debate about who should and who shouldn't come to live in Britain. This is something politicians have disagreed about for years.

ASYLUM SEEKERS CAUGHT IN BACK OF TRUCK IN DOVER

DESPERATE PEOPLE NEED OUR HELP WHOEVER THEY ARE

REFUGEES COSTING US TOO MUCH MONEY

OUR SCHOOLS AND HOSPITALS ARE OVERRUN WITH ILLEGALS!

REFUGEES ARRIVE ON THE SOUTH COAST FROM WAR-TORN CONGO

IF I GO BACK TO IRAQ, I WILL BE EXECUTED

These statements should open up the debate on the rights and wrongs of accepting people into Britain.

Before you complete the tasks, make sure you know the key terms.

An **asylum seeker** is a person who has made an application for asylum and is waiting to hear the decision on their application.

A **refugee** is someone who is recognised as a refugee under the UN 1951 Convention on Refugees and can remain in the country where they applied for asylum.

People in the UK can also be given **humanitarian protection**, meaning that the government believes that if they return to their country, their **human rights** will be infringed in an unacceptable way. Therefore, they are given rights to remain, and these rights are protected for five years, after which time they can be granted indefinite leave to remain if they still need protection.

People can also be refused asylum, but be given **discretionary leave** on compassionate or exceptional grounds, for example, a child who has spent their early years in the UK and has no ties with their parents' homeland. This is the most common form of leave given to unaccompanied asylum-seeking children. In these cases, the leave is for three years or until the person's eighteenth birthday. Anybody cleared to remain in the UK has the right to work, to legally have permanent accommodation and claim benefits.

The Basics

1. What is an asylum seeker? Give examples.
2. What is a refugee? Give examples.
3. What might the religion(s) you are studying say about refugees/asylum seekers? (Use the key concepts to help you.)
4. Research the topic of refugees. Find out about the terrible situations people find themselves in across the world today.
5. Have your findings influenced your views on people who arrive in Britain from other countries as refugees?

Case studies – what would you decide?

Task

1 a Read the four cases outlined below. In groups, decide which one you see as the most valid application for asylum in Britain.
  b Prepare a campaign for that person – a badge, a slogan, a religious angle and a persuasive speech to be used to fight for your person to be allowed to stay in Britain.
  c For the three you reject, list the problems you will be forcing these people to face as you return them to their own country.
  d Present your group's work to the rest of the class.
  e Finally, as a class, discuss the issues that were raised.

My story 1

My name is Salmaan and I arrived from Iran. I had to escape the country about six months ago. It's really hard for me to talk about it because in my country no one does talk about it and, in fact, people like me do not exist. You see, I'm gay and this is illegal in Iran. I can't help how I was born and I believe that as Allah created us all, he created me like this. I can't live a lie because this would be wrong, but I have lost my family as a result – they do not want to know me – it is as if I'm dead to them! I did have a partner in Iran, but a rumour started about him and he was arrested and, without a proper trial, was executed. I managed to flee the country and came to Britain. I'm a doctor, so I am willing to work, I'm not just here for the money or to sponge off everyone else. If you send me back, I will be arrested and executed too. You will be sending me to certain death.

My story 2

I lived in Rwanda, Africa. One day, my father woke us up in a panic. The government leader had been killed and the opposition rebels had seized power. They were from another tribe. Two days later, the genocide began! They came and ransacked the village. The old were rounded up, taken to a field and shot. I watched as my mother was gang raped. I will never get the image of fear in my mother's eyes out of my head.Children were treated the same – raped, murdered in killing fields. There was blood and death everywhere. The cattle were hacked to death. I fled, ran and ran and ran. I was ten at the time. I crossed the border into Tanzania with thousands of others. I worked in the sex industry to get some money and managed to pay a man to help me escape. To cut a long story short, here I am in Britain. I can't go back to that – my family are all probably dead.

My story 3

My name is Sanya – a 28-year-old Christian. I lived for 23 years in Afghanistan. I was an educated woman – a teacher. Then the Taliban arrived! They banned women from going to school, saying they don't need education. Music was banned, radio stations shut down, people were arrested for breaking Islamic law as they saw it. Life became harsh and miserable with regular executions of those who voiced any criticism. I wrote some articles in the newspapers because all of this was wrong. It's not Islam, it's power-crazed men. I was arrested and warned. One local officer, who was a friend of mine, came to warn me that they knew I was a Christian and so I was in great danger. I had no choice but to leave my country. I escaped via Pakistan and have an uncle living in Britain. I can't go back as they will kill me as a result of my religion.

My story 4

I'm a politician in Zimbabwe. I stand in total opposition to the government. I own a chain of factories and had published material to try to form a people's uprising. I spent five years in prison for speaking out. They tortured, beat, and abused me regularly. I managed to escape prison, but had to kill a guard to get out. I smuggled my way into Britain to claim asylum. If I go back, I will be arrested and executed for murder. I can safely campaign here and tell the world what is really going on. I can't go back! Death awaits me!

The list of problems that you produced in task c should have made you realise that no government decision is easy. Each has to be balanced by the fact that they cannot accept every asylum application or else the country would become unmanageable.

So now you know the issues about refugees and asylum seekers

The community spirit … engaging with multiculturalism

Abbas: What do we mean by community cohesion?

Minister: This a government initiative to try and bring people together. We provide money for specific projects.

Jan: Why is this necessary?

Minister: All over the country, we now have diverse communities and we need to help people to understand each other, and to bring about natural integration where people want to mix with each other not because they are forced to but by choice.

Paul: What kind of projects have you got in mind?

Minister: There are communities in Britain where there are people working hard to bring the faiths and cultures together to enable people to understand each other better and live in a more harmonious world. It is true that if we understood how people live and why they live that way, then we are more accepting. Societies which understand and accept everyone, get along more smoothly. Many communities have a mix of people and so there is work to be done. These projects help get rid of prejudice and discrimination – a major cause of problems in society. Many of the faith communities themselves are working to bring people together at leadership and local level.

Saira: How do you think religions can help?

Minister: Well, if we all understand each other's religion, then we start to understand their culture as well. It is up to the religions to make themselves open and inform and explain their beliefs to others. They need to bring people together because quite often religious principles are the ones that can lead to a better society. All religions believe in harmony, peace, tolerance and so on – they need to set the examples and so lead us all.

The Basics

1 What is meant by community cohesion?
2 Why is community cohesion an issue in Britain today?
3 **You cannot force people to mix**. What do you think? Explain your opinion.
4 Explain some of the ways that religion can try to bring people together.
5 Explain how the key concepts can help with the problem of community cohesion.
6 **Without religion there would be no community cohesion issues**. Do you agree? Give reasons for your answer, showing you have thought about more than one point of view. Refer to religious arguments in your answer.

Six religious projects

Buddhism 

In January 2008, the Buddhist Forum for Peace, Culture and Education met. It involved Buddhists, Muslims and black Christians. The participants have met regularly over the past six months in workshops. They have reflected on themselves, their backgrounds and the nature of their faith, and had frank discussions of stereotypes and assumptions they had about each other. This has enabled them to develop joint visions of how to transform their communities, workplaces and colleges.

Christianity 

The Bolton Christian Community Cohesion Project exists to inspire and encourage Christian organisations across the borough to fulfil their potential. It serves the different communities in Bolton including Christians, Muslims and Hindus by encouraging events that bring people together, and serve the local church by encouraging them to share with the wider community. The project offers a forum for the exchange of ideas, best practice and access to funding and volunteers.

Hinduism 

The Hindu Forum for Britain saw Ramesh Kallidai speak about the contributions made by migrants, and the shift of focus from multiculturalism to the building of good relations between the various communities that make up Britain. He spoke about integration and how this can be improved, how education can improve situations and how people can aspire to a better Britain. Members of the various faiths showed their commitment to moving forward.

Islam 

Wycombe Islamic Society (WISE) is committed to community cohesion and presenting the true Islam. It runs five-week courses to educate people about Islam, is part of the Sharing Faith initiative, uses the Building Bridges organisation and arranges visits to churches.

Judaism 

For the Jewish population in Britain, there are difficulties because of the issues in Israel and the Middle East today. In London in 2008, the Jewish Forum looked to improve Jewish life and how people understand them. It gave an outline of its proposed work with other faith communities in order to see how they can work together on matters of community cohesion through social responsibility schemes. The aim is to give young people confidence to mix without fear.

Sikhism 

The Sikh Religious and Interfaith Event 2008 in Leeds celebrated pride in the 800 years of the city. Living up to the 500-year-old Sikh tradition of 'langar', they prepared and served thousands of free vegetarian meals to all participants. This was inspired by their faith's founding principles to 'see God in all', promote 'unity in diversity', and put the qualities of compassion, generosity and selflessness into practice. There were interfaith activities to promote understanding in the city.

Now you have thought about community cohesion and religion

Celebration of religion and culture in Britain today

Festivals are a celebration of beliefs, cultures and traditions, expressed in the community for all to see. This is a really positive side to cultural differences and it is easy for people to mix together at these events, whether or not they are believers. The fact that people in Britain can openly celebrate, shows that most people accept our diverse culture. On the next three pages, you will learn about a festival from each of the six religions. The tasks appear at the end of the six festivals.

Wesak – Buddhism 

Wesak is the most important of the Buddhist festivals and is celebrated on the full moon in May. It celebrates the Buddha's birthday. 'Buddha' literally means 'one who is awake' and has become enlightened. To Buddhists, enlightenment is a blessed state in which the individual attains nirvana – the transcendence of desire and suffering.

The festival is really colourful and happy. Homes are cleaned and decorated and lanterns hung around the house. Buddhists visit their local temple for services and teaching, and give offerings to the monks of food, candles and flowers. Chanting and praying are an important part of Wesak. The 'Bathing the Buddha' ceremony is also often included. Water is poured over the shoulders of the Buddharupa (statue) and serves as a reminder to purify the mind from greed, hatred and ignorance.

Chinese Buddhists use their country's culture in their religious celebrations, for example, the traditional dancing dragons. Gifts are taken to an altar to be offered to the Buddha statues. This shows respect and gratitude to the Buddha for his life and teachings. If there is food, it is usually vegetarian as Buddhists try not to harm animals.

Christmas – Christianity 

This festival remembers the birth of Jesus and the events surrounding it. Jesus, for Christians, is the Son of God – sent by God to save humanity. Christmas in Britain is celebrated by many people, whether or not they are Christian. It has become a much commercialised celebration and some of the real message of it has been lost. However, most people get time off work and school and this gives them the opportunity to mix with others, send cards, buy presents and visit and celebrate with family. It is a time that brings everyone together. There is something to celebrate for everyone. For Christians, it is a very holy time with carol singing, church services, nativity plays, as well as family celebrations. As a Christian country, Christmas is part of the culture of Britain and allows people from other countries, who have settled here, to see and understand the basis of Christianity. People are able to share this belief with others.

Divali – Hinduism ॐ

Divali, the Hindu festival of lights, is the most popular of all the festivals from South Asia, and is also the occasion for celebrations by Jains and Sikhs as well as Hindus. In Britain, as in India, the festival is a time for thoroughly spring-cleaning the home and for wearing new clothes and, most importantly, decorating buildings with fancy lights.

Leicester has large Hindu and Sikh communities, and is known for its Divali celebrations. The festival of Divali extends over five days. It's a great favourite with children because of the lights, fireworks and sweets involved. For Hindus, the festival remembers the story of the God Rama and his wife Sita and their battle with the demon Ravanna. It celebrates the victory of good over evil, light over darkness and knowledge over ignorance. Whether or not you believe in the story of Rama and Sita, what is important is that the lights stand for a year of hope, a commitment to goodwill and friendship to all and the joy that good action can bring. This can be shared with all people.

Id-ul-Fitr – Islam 

The festival of Id-ul-Fitr falls at the end of the holy month of Ramadan. Muslims are not only celebrating the end of fasting, but thanking Allah for the help and strength that he gave them throughout the previous month to help them practise self-control. The festival begins when the first sight of the new moon is seen in the sky.

Muslims in most countries rely on news of an official sighting, rather than looking at the sky themselves. The celebratory atmosphere is increased by everyone wearing best or new clothes, and decorating their homes. There are special services out of doors and in mosques, processions through the streets and, of course, a special celebratory meal eaten during daytime – the first daytime meal Muslims will have had in a month. Restaurants are booked out for extended family gatherings. These often spill out on to the streets with everyone partying together. People send each other cards and presents, and visit cemeteries to remember lost loved ones.

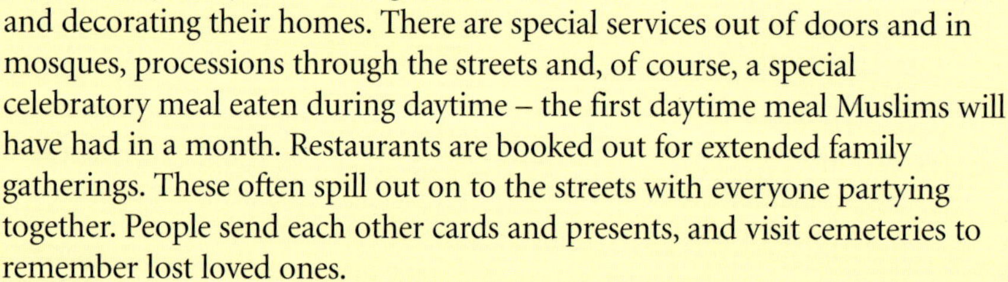

However, on a more serious level, Id is also a time of forgiveness, and making amends for wrong doings. Most of what is done in Islam is done privately – in the mosques or in Makkah on Hajj – so Id is a chance to express religious celebration openly. It allows others to see something of the religion and, therefore, understand it better.

Pesach – Judaism

Pesach is the festival of Passover, remembering the saving of the Jews (Israelites) from slavery in Egypt. With the help of Moses, the ten plagues and the death of every firstborn son, the escape was possible. The Talmud states that 'everyone has to imagine that he/she was a slave and has now emerged from their personal Egypt'. These words form a part of the seder meal. The festival lasts for eight days with the first and last two being days of rest. The house is cleaned of yeast and children usually go on a Chametz yeast hunt to make sure that the house is free of it.

In relation to the other religions, Pesach is low key in terms of being celebrated in the community. It is mainly focused on the home and the synagogue, rather than flowing into the streets of Britain. Perhaps this reflects the importance of the family in Judaism, but also the persecution Jewish people have had to face over the centuries.

Baisaiki – Sikhism 

Sikhs celebrate this New Year festival in April and it commemorates 1699 when Sikhism really began as a religion, with the start of the Khalsa. It was a harvest festival in the Punjab before Sikhs added their religious dimension to it. Gurdwaras are decorated and there are parades along the streets, dancing and singing of hymns and scriptures throughout the day. Processions will be led by members of the Khalsa and five men dressed as the Panj Pyares. The Guru Granth Sahib is carried through the streets. In 2008, the prime minister joined the Baisaiki celebrations in an Essex gurdwara, during which he praised the Sikhs and said that the Sikh principles of tolerance, equality and treating people with fairness are virtues that all communities should work hard to make real.

Task

1. Explain why the religion(s) you have studied celebrate their festival(s).
2. Explain how the religion(s) you have studied celebrate their festival(s).
3. What does it say about British society that all religions are free to celebrate their festivals in Britain?
4. How do festivals help us to understand the different religions?
5. **Multiculturalism is working in Britain and the festival celebrations clearly show this.** Do you agree? Give reasons for your answer, showing you have thought about more than one point of view. Refer to religious arguments in your answer.

Now you know about religious festivals in Britain today

Exam tips

Candidates – that's you – often find answering evaluative questions difficult when they feel strongly about the statement given and can't see the other side of the argument. So this topic is a prime case where this might happen. Usually such candidates go on and on about the statement being right or wrong, so here are some helpful tips to prevent you from throwing away valuable marks.

1 Read the statement carefully and underline the key words – this will steer your brain in the right direction. Make sure that you are answering the question that has been set.
2 Write the statement out on your answer page – your brain processes it a bit better, and you are more likely to answer it.
3 Each time you pause when you are writing, recheck the statement so that you are still answering it.
4 Double-check you have agreed and disagreed, whatever your personal opinion is.
5 Double-check you have some religion in your answer.

Examiner's comments

Tom has given a one-sided argument with a little bit of explanation. It is worth 2 marks.

Jake has misread the question – he saw the word 'work' and that led him in his answer – no marks. Do you think he recognises the term 'multiculturalism'? This shows why it is important to learn all the technical words for the course.

Sarah has written an answer that gives both sides, but no religious comment and little explanation. She has restricted herself to 3 marks.

Taylor has made one valid point, but it makes no sense to have a go at the exam question in your answer! Stick to answering the question and avoid letting them irritate you (or you might irritate the person marking it!).

Don't forget that if you decide to criticise the writer of the question, it might be your hard luck to have that person as your examiner! Examiners never, ever write what they really think – they are just trying to get you to argue.

Advice desk

Okay, read the sample answers below and imagine you are trying to teach other students how to improve in their exams – what's gone wrong? Give them some good advice.

The question was:

Multiculturalism does not work in Britain. Do you agree? Give reasons for your answer, showing you have thought about more than one point of view. Refer to religious arguments in your answer. *(6 marks)*

Sample answers

Tom –

I don't agree with that. All places have people of different colours and from different religions. They aren't fighting all the time. So it does work.

Jake –

I agree with the statement, it's true. There is just too much unemployment now, so people don't have jobs – no work.

Sarah –

We are the ones who should know. If you look in your community you wouldn't know what country you were in these days – all different religious buildings, all different fast-food places. Curry is now more popular than fish and chips! People live with people of their own kind, not mixing with others, but this is what people want. So I disagree and agree really.

Taylor –

Of course it works! We live in one without that much trouble. Stupid question really.

These answers could be genuine – the authors of this book have seen their equivalents every year!

Topic Five Religion and identity

The road of life.

In this topic you are going to be exploring the place of the individual within society, the global community and religious traditions. You will be looking at important questions related to the human condition. Some of these relate to what it means to be human, the difference between the physical and **spiritual dimensions** to life. You will also be exploring the nature of **ultimate questions** and considering how religious traditions help people to make sense of these and find answers to the purpose and meaning of life.

You will need to be familiar with the key teachings of the religions you are studying and use these to explore religious attitudes to the issues raised. You will examine how religious belief contributes to the **identity** of the individual within the **faith community**; how commitment is demonstrated in many ways, such as ceremonies, traditions, **symbolism** and lifestyle; and the choices that individuals make and the guidance that their beliefs offer them in the decision-making process.

It is fair to say that we are all very complex individuals and it is impossible to know everything about someone, no matter how close we are to them. In fact, there are lots of things we do not really know for certain about ourselves. Life has often been described as a journey of self-discovery. As we grow older and have more experiences, our personalities develop and mature, we learn more about ourselves and others. For many religious people, this life is a test and their responses to the many challenges that life presents are all part of a preparation for a future eternal life in heaven, or will influence their next life when reincarnated.

Think about yourself for a moment. What can someone know about you just by your appearance? What can you tell about people by looking at them? How could you get to know more about them?

Task

Draw an illustrated life map to show the progress of your life up to now. Then extend it by adding some of the things that may happen to you in the future. For example, you have already been born, learned to walk, started school. In the future you may go to university, buy your first home and get married.

Who am I?

How would you answer this question?

Who am I? Discuss your ideas with a partner.

The question could be answered by looking at the chemical composition of living things. Everyone is made up of a complex construction of matter that could be broken down into many different elements. For example, it has been speculated that in every human being there is enough iron to make an eight inch nail and enough carbon to make 2000 pencils. Look at the image of Mr and Mrs Chemistry.

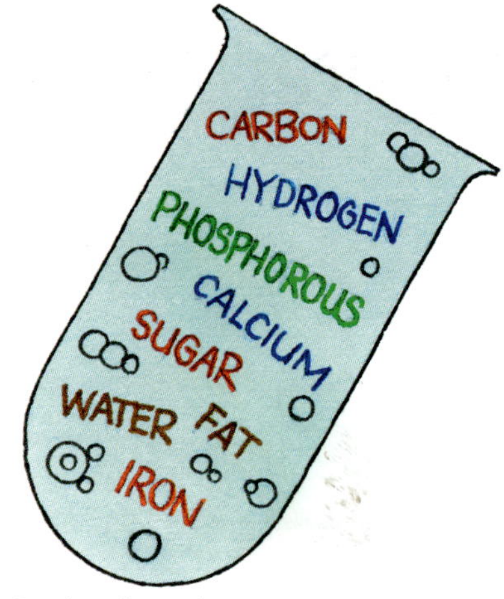

Recipe for a human.

Is this really all we are? What is missing?

Some people would say that we are simply another species of animal living on earth. Certainly we share some characteristics with other mammals. You may be familiar with the acrostic MRS GREN from your biology lessons. All living organisms have the following:

- Movement.
- Respiration.
- Sensitivity.
- Growth.
- Reproduction.
- Excretion.
- Nutrition.

But how are we different from other animals?

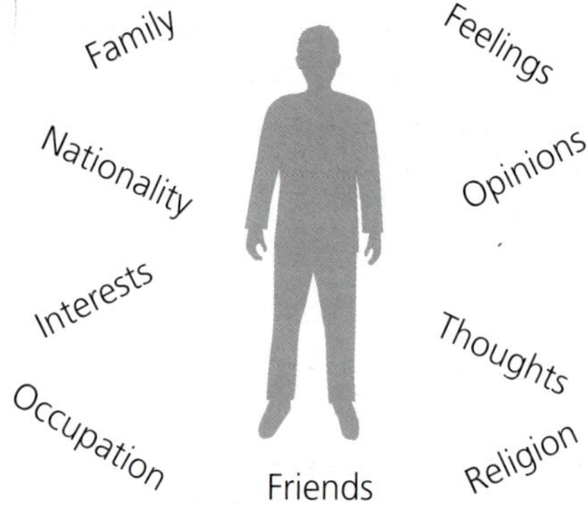

Who we are is made up of many things. You may be a son or daughter, a hockey player, a musician, a friend and an optimist. One way to answer the question is to consider all the things that contribute to making us unique individuals. If you consider the points in the diagram, you will see that we all have many different aspects to ourselves and that, throughout our lives, we constantly grow and change.

Some would say that it is these differences that make humanity unique amongst the animal world. Certainly, within all religious traditions, human life is valued highly. In Christianity, Islam and Judaism there is the belief that each individual has been created by God. In Buddhism, Hinduism and Sikhism it is believed that the human form must be attained before there can be release from the cycle of reincarnation.

Task

Let's think about who we are. Copy and add to the following table. Try to add at least three examples under each heading.

Groups	Feelings	Opinions	Interests
English	Anger	Environmentalist	Football

The Basics

1. How could you answer the question: 'Who am I?'
2. What makes human beings similar to animals?
3. How are human beings different from animals?
4. Why do you think religious teachings consider human life to be the highest?
5. **Religious people are wrong to say humans are more important than animals.** What do you think? Explain your opinion.

Now you have thought about what makes up a human

Physical and spiritual dimensions to life

We have seen that there is no simple answer to the question: 'Who am I?' It is possible to describe people in many ways. What is apparent is that there appears to be an indefinable quality about human beings that sets us apart from all other forms of life. Every person is a unique and complex individual. Even identical twins will have physical differences, such as thumbprints, and their personal qualities will almost certainly ensure that people who know them can always tell them apart.

The physical dimension

Everyone has a body – it is the means through which we experience life. Everything we do in life is, in part, dictated by our physical being. Our bodies influence us to some extent. For example, becoming a world-class athlete requires physical attributes as well as talent and determination. For religious people, the body is special and should be looked after and cared for. Within religious traditions there are often rules and practices to encourage believers to keep a healthy body.

The spiritual dimension

It is often easiest to think of the spiritual dimension of a person as the inner being or unique qualities of each individual. Everyone can think, have feelings and emotions. We wonder about the world around us and search for answers to questions about the meaning and purpose of life. It is our ability to reflect upon and evaluate our actions that enables us to choose to grow and develop as more complete human beings.

All religious traditions teach that human beings are very special. They all emphasise the sanctity of human life and (with the exception of Buddhism) that all people are important to God. This means that religious teachings are concerned not only with the physical life on earth, but also with the spiritual growth and development of believers. Life is seen as a gift and should be respected.

Each person is more than just a physical body; they have a unique, invisible quality, often referred to as a spirit, soul or atman. This is the true lasting part of every individual. The body will one day die, but the spirit of the person will live on.

One way to understand how the physical and spiritual come together is to think of the way people see us. Our outer physical layer is apparent to everyone who looks at us. People may form judgements about what kind of person we are simply from our appearance. When people speak to us, they get to know a little more and they can start to form opinions about us based on more than just what we look like. However, to really understand someone, we need to spend a lot of time with them, in different situations and environments. Think about this for a moment – who really knows you well? Why?

Task

Draw an outline of a Russian doll. Around the outside, write words that describe your physical appearance. On the inside, write words that describe your personality.

The Basics

1. What is meant by the physical dimension to life?
2. What is meant by the spiritual dimension to life?
3. **Religious people should value the spiritual side of life more than the physical.** What do you think? Explain your opinion.

Now you have thought about spiritual and physical dimensions

Ultimate questions

Does God exist?
How long was the Tudor dynasty?
When is Valentine's Day?
Who started the Khalsa?
Should I do what is right?
Where is Puerto Rico?
Was Jesus the Son of God?
Why is there suffering in the world?
What is on the TV tonight?
Can miracles be performed?
Can I get a train from Sunderland to Glasgow?
Does salt dissolve?
Is there a heaven?
Is there a purpose to life?
What happens when you die?
What do I need to make a chicken curry?
Which team is at the top of the premiership?
Are we reincarnated?
How do you play Scrabble?
Why am I here?

Read the questions above. Sort them into two categories.

When you read the questions, it would have soon become apparent that there is a difference between them. Some of the questions are everyday questions that we ask all the time. They have straightforward answers. Even if we don't know the answers to them, there are many different sources of information that could be used to find the answers. We could ask an expert, look on the internet or perform an experiment. We could find the answers in many ways and be confident that we have the correct response.

The other group of questions is quite different. These questions deal with issues of a much more challenging and personal nature. Whilst you may well spend lunchtime discussing the football results or fashion, it is very unlikely that you would routinely discuss the meaning of life! These questions tend to only be discussed when we are in a more serious frame of mind or when something happens that challenges us to question the world in which we live. For example, if someone we love and care for is tragically killed, it would be natural to question whether there is justice in the world or why they have been taken from us. Sometimes world events, such as wars and natural disasters, may make us question the purpose of suffering and the existence of a loving God.

These questions are called ultimate questions because they deal with issues and concerns that have troubled humanity from earliest times. In every society and culture there is evidence of humanity's attempts to find answers to questions about the meaning and purpose of life, and human life in particular. For example, we know that the ancient Egyptians believed in a life after death that would be similar to life on earth – why else would they bury their dead with the artefacts of life on earth?

For many people, the answers to these questions lie in their religious beliefs and traditions. Religious faith provides believers with a structure to their lives and answers questions through the sacred writings, prophets, traditions, and so on.

But why do you think people want answers to these questions?

The Basics

1 List some differences between the two groups of question.
2 What is meant by the term 'ultimate questions'?
3 How could people find answers to ultimate questions?
4 Why do people not agree on the answers to ultimate questions?
5 **Ultimate questions are the most important questions to ask.** What do you think? Explain your opinion.

Now you know the term 'ultimate questions'

Identity in a faith community

The faith community can be compared to a family, where all the members share similar goals and aspirations. Being a part of the community gives the individual a sense of belonging and this may be expressed through many customs and traditions. For example, membership of the community may require a person to wear special dress, follow specific rules or attend certain ceremonies. There are many reasons why people choose to commit to a religious faith, but ultimately, it will be because it gives them a sense of meaning and purpose in their lives.

In some religious traditions there is the option to commit completely to a religious way of life and leave the material world behind. The monastic movements found in Buddhism and Christianity offer a lifestyle choice to individuals who want to devote their lives to prayer and religious practice. Hindu sadhus leave behind all worldly possessions to live a life devoted to spiritual practices.

In all religious traditions the family is an important social group where children often gain their religious identity. It is here that they will learn about their faith during everyday life. Parents will introduce their children to the religious teachings and beliefs. They will celebrate important festivals together, pray and worship together at home and at their local place of worship. They will encourage their children to adopt and practise the values and morality of their faith.

Research Task

For one religion that you are studying, research how belonging to the community may affect a person's life. Present your findings in a leaflet: 'My life as a (insert name of religion)'.

Religious leaders

In all religious traditions there are leaders who guide and support members in their faith. They are chosen in different ways depending on the religion, but they are usually people who the rest of the community respect for their piety and knowledge. The leader's role is principally to conduct worship and lead ceremonies. They may also offer important pastoral support. They will usually have responsibility for the place of worship and help the community to provide services such as prayer groups, youth fellowship and social activities. The leaders will go out into the community where needed, for example, visiting the sick and elderly or acting as school governors and participating in local council groups.

Find out more about the role of a religious leader.
If possible, invite someone to come and talk to your class about their work.

The Basics

1 Why do you think people become members of faith communities?
2 What are the advantages for a person choosing to become a monk or nun?
3 **Becoming a monk or nun is the best way to become close to God**. Do you agree? Give reasons for your answer, showing you have thought about more than one point of view. Refer to religious arguments in your answer.

Now you have thought about religious identity

Ceremonies of commitment

Most religious traditions have ceremonies where young people make a personal commitment to the faith. These occur at different times, but usually around the teenage years, so they are sometimes referred to as coming-of-age ceremonies. They mark the change from childhood to adulthood. After this, young people are expected to take full responsibility for their religious duties.

Buddhism 

There is no specific ceremony to become a Buddhist. Some will repeat the Three Refuges in front of others to mark their acceptance of the Buddhist way of life. This is because the Buddha taught that it is the way you live that is important. The believer will simply state, 'I go to the Buddha for refuge; I go to the dharma for refuge; I go to the sangha for refuge.'

In Theravada Buddhism, an important ceremony marks a young person's entry into a monastery. Before entering the wat (monastery), the young man must be free from debt and know the Pali phrases he must say in the ceremony. He visits the wat several times and makes gifts of incense, flowers and light, and rings a gong showing he is preparing to join the monastery. The day before the ceremony, he walks in a procession wearing a white robe symbolising his good and pure intentions in becoming a monk. His head is shaved.

On his initiation day, he walks around the wat four times wearing rich clothing and carrying a candle, incense and flower. He takes off the rich clothes and throws coins on the floor, to symbolise the actions of

Christianity 

Around the age of twelve, many young Christians choose to undergo a ceremony of confirmation. This is when they confirm the promises made for them at their baptism. Before the ceremony, there is a time of preparation when they will attend classes, learning what it means to make a full commitment to the Christian faith and how they should live a Christian life.

In Anglican Churches, the ceremony takes place at a special Sunday service, led by a bishop. The bishop will ask three questions: 'Do you turn to Christ? Do you repent your sins? Do you renounce evil?' Each time, the person must answer 'Yes'. The bishop then places his hands on their head and says: 'Confirm O Lord your servant with your Holy Spirit.' This is called the laying on of hands, and at this point, the young person receives the blessing of God's Holy Spirit to guide them

Hinduism ॐ

In Hinduism, sixteen samskaras (special ceremonies) mark key events in a person's life. At around the age of twelve, Hindu boys have a sacred thread ceremony to mark their full entry into their caste. The ceremony happens in a garden around a sacred fire. Puja (worship) is conducted and then the boy's teacher presents him with his sacred thread, which is a series of cotton threads twined together.

The priest who has taught the boy, then places the sacred thread over the boy's left shoulder and across his body to the right hip. He is now allowed to recite passages from the Vedas and conduct religious rituals. In due course, he is also now ready for the next stage in life – marriage.

rince Siddhartha when he left the alace for the last time. He then enters ıe ordination hall and asks the hikkus (monks) to ordain him. He puts on simple yellow robes to show that he has left his worldly life behind. The abbot asks him questions and he must answer in Pali. He is then accepted into the monastery and his religious instruction begins.

ı their Christian life. The service then ontinues with Holy Communion and ıe newly-confirmed person receives ıe bread and wine for the first time.

Believer's baptism

In the Baptist Church, they do not baptise children. They wait until a young person feels ready to understand the commitment they are making. In church, they announce that they are sorry for the sins they have committed and accept Christ as their personal saviour. The minister then leads them into the baptistery and dips them completely under the water.

This symbolises the washing away of sins and rising to a new life in Christ.

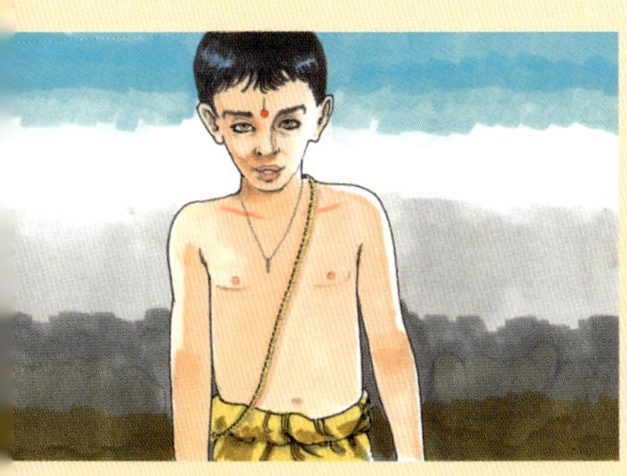

The Basics

1 Describe a commitment ceremony and explain the meaning of any symbolic words, actions and objects.
2 Why do you think these ceremonies of commitment are sometimes called coming-of-age ceremonies?
3 Why do some religious people think it is important to have these ceremonies?
4 Give three ways a believer's life would be affected after becoming a full member of their faith community.
5 **Initiation ceremonies are pointless because your religion is decided at birth**. Do you agree? Give reasons for your answer, showing you have thought about more than one point of view. Refer to religious arguments in your answer.

Islam

There are no ceremonies of commitment in Islam as a child is considered a full Muslim from birth. Islam is a complete way of life and children learn their faith in the family and in the madrasah (mosque school) as they grow up.

The words of the Bismillah mean 'In the name of God, most gracious, most compassionate'

When a Muslim child is four, they have a ceremony called Bismillah. It remembers the first time Prophet Muhammad (pbuh) met the angel Gabriel, when he was commanded to read the first words of the Qur'an from a scroll presented by the angel. The child will have memorised the passage known as the Bismillah and recites it for family and friends to

Judaism

At the age of thirteen, all Jewish boys have a ceremony called Bar Mitzvah, which means 'son of the commandment'. In Reform Judaism, girls have a ceremony called Bat Mitzvah, which means 'daughter of the commandment', and is completed when they are

twelve. These are very important ceremonies because they mark the change from child to adult. From this point, the young person is completely responsible for their religious duties.

There is a period of preparation during which a rabbi will instruct the young boy in how to read and handle the Torah, as well as how to perform other religious

Sikhism

When Sikh boys and girls are old enough, they can choose to be initiated into the Khalsa through the Amrit ceremony. However, it is very common for Sikhs to leave this ceremony until much later in life. Guru Gobind Singh invented this ceremony in 1699 and it involves making a commitment to live by a very strict moral

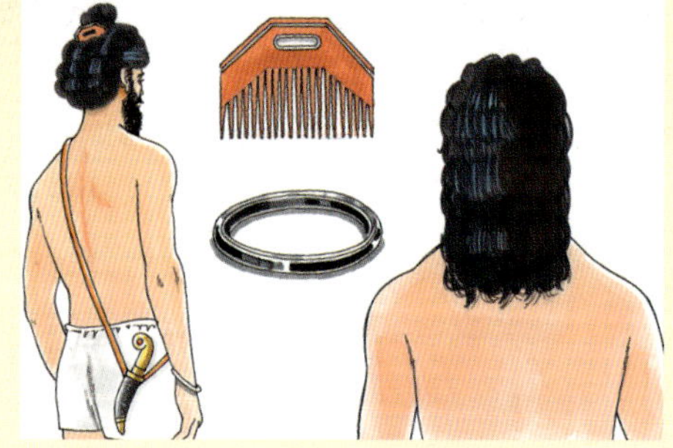

The 5Ks

code, including adopting all of the 5Ks.

The Amrit ceremony is conducted in front of the Guru Granth Sahib. There are five members dressed to represent the Panj Pyare (five beloved ones). The granthi reads from the holy book and one of the Panj Pyare recites the vows the initiates must promise to keep. The amrit, a mixture of sugar and water, is stirred with a Khanda – double-edged sword. The initiates kneel

hear. They receive gifts of sweets. This marks the beginning of their religious education.

As they get older, they take on more of the religious duties. They learn how to prepare for and complete prayers so that they can fulfil Salah – the Second Pillar of Islam. Many Muslim children keep the full Ramadan fast by the time they are in their early teens, thus completing Sawm – the Fourth Pillar of Islam.

obligations, such how to wear tefillin. The ceremony takes place on the Sabbath nearest to the boy's thirteenth birthday as part of the usual service at the synagogue. The Torah scrolls are prepared on the bimah and then the rabbi calls the boy to read to the rest of the congregation. The boy goes up to the bimah and reads the passages in Hebrew for that Shabbat service.

The rabbi then gives his sermon, part of this is for the boy, to remind him of his duty to keep the commandments throughout his life. Finally, the boy is blessed by the rabbi with the words: 'The Lord bless thee and keep thee.' Then there is a big family celebration.

on one knee to show that they are ready to defend their faith. Amrit is then sprinkled on their eyes and hair to the words 'Waheguru ji ka Khalsa', which means the 'Khalsa is the chosen of God'. Those being baptised reply, 'Waheguru ji ki fateh', which means 'victory to God'. Each person drinks some of the amrit from the bowl, to show equality and the absence of castes.

There are then prayers and hymns and the ceremony closes with the sharing of karah parshad (blessed food). After the ceremony, all Sikh men take the name Singh, meaning lion, and

women take the name Kaur, meaning princess.

Now you know about commitment ceremonies

Religion and identity

A Buddhist

I am a Buddhist. The teachings and lifestyle of the Buddha have given me guidance on the direction my life should take. My faith gives me a way of behaving and living, and I find it helps me make decisions that keep me in harmony with the world. I meditate every day and this gives me a sense of peace that carries through all day. My friends know I am a Buddhist, so do not offer me alcohol and tobacco. As I live in a Western society, most people would not recognise that I am a Buddhist as I do not wear the traditional robes that Buddhist monks and nuns wear in sanghas all over the world. I meet twice a week with my Buddhist friends at a yoga and meditation class, as there are no holy buildings in my locality.

A Christian

I am a Christian and I try to live my life following the example of Jesus and the teachings of the Bible. I sometimes wear a crucifix as a symbol of my faith and I have an ichthus, which is a fish shape, on my car. My faith guides the way I behave and live my life. I attend church every week and help out at the Sunday school. On Wednesdays, I sometimes lead the prayer group that meets each week in different people's homes. I find that most people have respect for my religious beliefs and I am fortunate to be living in the UK because it means that holidays coincide with the main festivals that I celebrate. Sometimes, however, it can be difficult practising my faith as many people in today's society don't always understand how important God is in my life. At school, I remember that I tended to not say anything about my faith because a lot of my classmates thought religion wasn't very cool.

A Hindu

I am a Hindu. Many people are aware of my religious beliefs because I wear traditional Indian dress and the tilak mark on my forehead is often recognised. I find it easy to practise my faith in the UK because I perform the family puja every day in my home. I have a shrine in the kitchen where we can perform our religious duties. As a Hindu, I have chosen to follow a vegetarian lifestyle because of my belief in ahimsa. I am fortunate to live in an area where we have a temple and the main services take place on a Sunday, so my family and I are able to attend. Mostly, I find that people are very interested in my religion and, when we have special celebrations like Divali and Holi, lots of people in the community come to the celebrations even if they are not Hindus.

Task

Read the statements below. With a partner, take it in turns to give different reasons to agree with each one. Then do the same for disagreeing. Make it tougher (but better preparation for the exam) by challenging each other to explain their point and/or to give an example.

a Religious people should always put their religion first.
b Wearing s religious symbol tells everyone of your beliefs.
c Worship is the most important part of being religious.

A Muslim

I am a Muslim and my faith is very important to me. The holy Qur'an gives me all the instructions I need to live my life correctly. It is not always possible to make the prayers during the day because I work as a paramedic, but I do try to complete them during my breaks. I find that this helps me to remember that my purpose is to serve Allah throughout the day and this gives me a sense of peace. My colleagues are very supportive of me during Ramadan and some have even done the fast with me for a day to raise funds for the service. My local community mosque is a conversion of a number of houses. It is an important place for us as it allows us to gather and worship together. We are currently raising funds for a new mosque that will be designed using traditional architecture.

A Jew

I am an Orthodox Jew and many people recognise this from my appearance. I wear the sides of my hair long because it is commanded in the Torah. When I go out, I wear a traditional long black overcoat and hat. Some people do look at me oddly if they are unaware of why I am dressed in this way. If people ask about my dress or about the mezuzah they see when they come to the front door, I always explain. I have never been embarrassed by this because my faith is an important part of my identity. As a Jew, I am guided by the teachings of the Torah and I try to stick to these because they give meaning and purpose to my life. Friday evening is especially important in my home because it is the start of Shabbat. This is our day of rest and is a valuable part of family life. During Shabbat, we spend time as a family in worship and enjoy each other's company. On Saturday morning, we attend worship together in the synagogue.

A Sikh

I am a Sikh and I took the decision to become a full member of the community when I was eighteen. This meant that I made a commitment to represent my faith and community, as well as to adopt a lifestyle that gives me direction in my life. As a member of the Khalsa, I have vowed to wear the Five Ks, which means that everyone can see that I am a Sikh. I am very proud of my traditions and am honoured to be a part of the community. It is important to me to attend the gurdwara regularly where I am able to contribute to the community as a musician and by performing sewa in the langar. Family life is an important part of my faith and, as the youngest son, I have my mother living with me since she was widowed. This has been a great help to my wife who has been able to resume her career knowing that our children are well cared for at home.

The Basics

1. Make a poster explaining some of the symbols of faith that might be:
   - a worn by a member of the faith
   - b found in the home of a religious believer.
2. Explain how being a member of a faith community may affect the everyday life of a believer.
3. **Religious people should not wear symbols of their faith**. What do you think? Explain your opinion.

Now you have thought about religion and identity

Religious attitudes to healthy living

All religious traditions teach that we are all special and unique in some way. This is summed up in the teaching of the sanctity of life. The physical body is seen as a shell that carries the real inner person. Within all religious traditions, there are beliefs and practices that encourage believers to care not only for others, but for themselves. Spiritual growth can only be achieved if a person is healthy physically and mentally.

How might religious belief and practice help someone have a healthy mind and body?

- Morality – all religious traditions encourage people to live their lives honestly and with respect for others. This will help them to avoid conflict and achieve a sense of peace.
- Meditation – the practice of meditation helps to clear and focus the mind, helping a person to achieve a sense of peace and tranquillity.
- Discipline – all religious traditions have rules and practices to encourage self-discipline. This may include not using drugs, performing daily rituals, going on pilgrimage, and so on.
- Community – being part of a faith community gives people a sense of belonging and responsibility. The community will also support people when they are having problems.
- Prayer – regular prayers help believers to think about their values and about what is important to them. They know there is always someone there for them when life gets hard.
- Confession – it can be very upsetting to do something wrong and have it weighing on your mind. Through confession, a believer can ease their conscience and demonstrate that they are truly penitent (sorry). They may do this in personal meditation or seek the support of a religious leader.
- Lifestyle – all religions encourage believers to live their lives by a code of conduct that will encourage them to care for themselves and others.

The Basics

1. Explain the teaching of the sanctity of life.
2. Explain two ways that religious practices can help a believer to have:
   a. a healthy body
   b. a healthy mind.
3. **Religious people should not do anything that could damage their bodies.** What do you think? Explain your opinion.

Buddhism 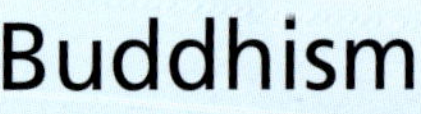 

'Health is the greatest of gifts.
(The Dhammapada)

Christianity 

'Each of you should learn to control your own body in a way that is holy and honourable.'
(1 Thessalonians 4:4)

Hinduism 

'Yoga destroys suffering for him who is moderate in eating, leisure activities, work, sleep and wakefulness.'
(Bhagavad Gita)

Islam 

'We give through this [Qur'an] all that gives health and is a grace to those who believe.
(Qur'an)

Judaism 

'This [G-d's teaching] will bring health to your body and nourishment to your bones.
(Proverbs 3:8)

Sikhism 

'The pain of selfishness is gone. I have found peace, my body has become healthy.
(Guru Granth Sahib)

Decision making

Read the following situations. What would you do in each case? Decide your answer to a, before you read b.

1 a You are standing in a queue waiting to be served when you see someone take a purse from a lady's bag while she is not looking.

b Would you react the same if the thief was shoplifting?

2 a Your parents are going away for the weekend and your friends are urging you to have a party. Your parents have said you must not have anyone in the house.

b You have the party and someone takes your dad's prized signed football.

3 a Your friend wants your advice because she thinks she is pregnant. She asks you to keep quiet about it.

b Your friend's boyfriend suspects something and asks you what is going on.

4 a In assembly, you are told that someone has taken a laptop belonging to your favourite teacher. You know who did it and they know you are the only one who saw them.

b Would you react differently if you did not like or know the teacher?

How did you decide what to do in each case? Do you think that all your actions were the right thing to do? What influences your decisions?

From the moment we are born we begin a process of socialisation. We start to learn the behaviour and attitudes that are expected from us in society. An important part of this process is learning the difference between right and wrong. At first, we do this in our families, but as we grow and develop we encounter many different influences and have to start to decide for ourselves what is right for us. After all, on many issues, it isn't always clear-cut what is the right thing to do.

Morality concerns issues of right and wrong. Human beings have the capacity to think about their actions and make decisions about the way they should behave. Our sense of what is right and wrong is determined by all the influences upon us. Furthermore, what we consider right, someone else may think is wrong. Therefore, making moral judgements can be very difficult.

Influences

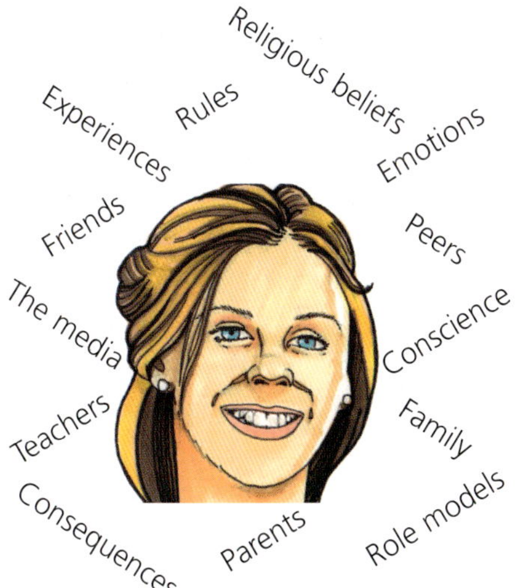

Write a sentence that explains each of these influences. Can you think of any more? Which influences do you think are the most important and why?

For many people, their religion is an important influence on their moral judgements. They will be especially influenced by their sacred writings, religious leaders and conscience when making moral choices. For example, Roman Catholic teaching states that abortion is wrong; a Muslim believes the Qur'an to be the exact Word of Allah. When people choose to be part of a faith, they take on all aspects of that faith and, consequently, it will have a huge impact on the way they live their lives.

The Basics

1 Explain how a person's religion can help them to make decisions.

2 **You should always do the right thing**. Do you agree? Give reasons for your answer, showing you have thought about more than one point of view. Refer to religious arguments in your answer.

Now you have explored decision making

Multiple identities

Are you the same in every situation? Read the following speech bubbles. How and why do these young people change who they are?

I prefer to be on my own at home and school, but when my family visits relatives I have to speak respectfully and do stuff with them.

Abas

In school, I work hard and some of my classmates think I'm a swot. But when I'm with my mates, you'd better watch out! I have a great time.

Jem

When I go to the football with my dad, I don't know what happens! I get really loud and argumentative, shouting at the team and the ref. Bizarre! I am normally very quiet.

Bill

We all behave differently in different situations and with different people because the circumstances demand this of us. It means we can be said to have **multiple identities**.

But what about our identity as part of a community? What makes us a good citizen? Do we have multiple identities here?

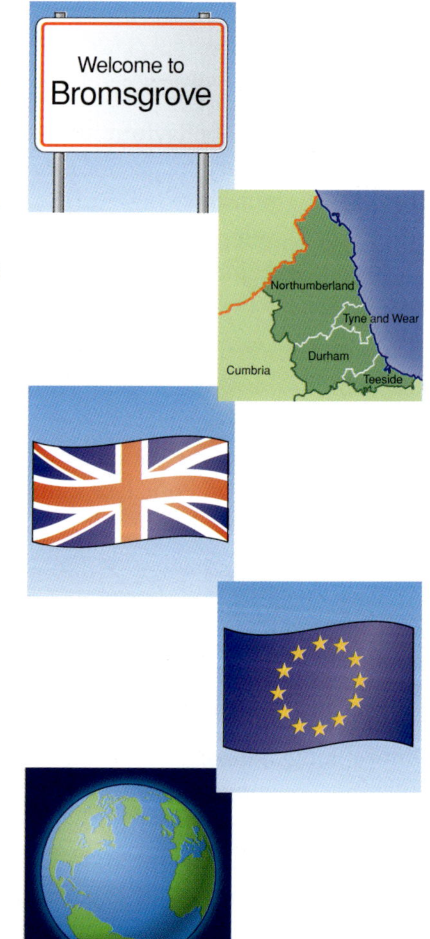

Local community – we all live in a locality, it's probably where we go to school, work and spend much of our leisure time. *Is it important to contribute to our local community? What can we do to make our locality a good place to live?*

Regional community – your local community will be part of a wider regional community. You might live in the West Midlands or the north east of England. *What is special about your part of the country? What marks you out? Is it important to you that people recognise where you are from? What contribution can you make to your region?*

National identity – the UN Charter emphasises that everyone has a right to a nationality. *What does being British mean to you? Can you identify characteristics that people would say are typical of someone who is English, Irish, Scottish or Welsh? Do we have a responsibility to represent our country when we travel abroad on holiday, for example?*

European identity – since the UK is in Europe and part of the European Community, we can all be said to be European. *What does this mean to you? How is being European different to coming from some other continent in the world?*

Global identity – we are all members of the human race, which means we have responsibilities to all humans and to the planet we live on, doesn't it? *What might these responsibilities be?*

On every level, religions get involved – all say you have a duty to your fellow man, as well as to the world and to the worldwide community. *How are the religious faiths involved at these different levels? Find out about some of the ways religious believers have contributed to issues at local, national and international level.*

Now you have thought about the different groups you belong to

Exam practice

Exam Tip

Stimulus material is provided to help you orientate your responses, so it is worth spending a few moments studying the material provided. In the exam question below, the pictures provide a direct link to the first question. They give you a clue as to how you should approach the answer. How can the stimulus help you to write a good response?

Time test

As you get near to the exam, it is important to practise writing timed answers to the exam question. You need to allow time in the exam to settle down, read the paper and have time to check through your answers at the end of the exam. This means you have about 20 minutes to complete a question. Remember to look at the marks available for each part of the question. They will help you to judge how much you need to write and, therefore, how long to spend on a question. If the question part is worth 1 mark, you don't need to write a five-minute essay.

It is important not to rush through your answers; you do have time to complete them well. It is worth spending a few moments thinking about your answer to a question before actually rushing to write it down. Some questions are only short-answer responses and will not take very long. Questions asking you to describe, explain or give opinions and reasons will take more time. These questions will need you to think through your answer first. It might be worth making a few pencilled notes planning your response if it's a question you find difficult.

Take the time test

Complete the exam question below in 20 minutes.

1. Religion and identity

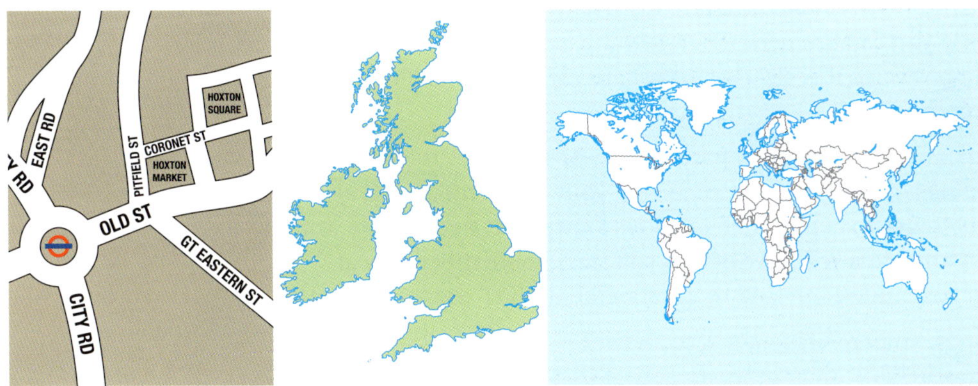

(a) Briefly explain what is meant by the term 'multiple identity'. *(2 marks)*

(b) Explain some of the ways that religious belief can help people make decisions in their lives. *(3 marks)*

(c) 'Religion does not give people answers to questions about the purpose of life.'
Do you agree? Explain your opinion. *(3 marks)*

(d) Describe a ceremony of commitment in **one** religion you have studied. *(4 marks)*

(e) 'There are more important things in life than being a religious believer.'
Do you agree? Give reasons for your answer, showing you have thought about more than one point of view. Refer to religious arguments in your answer. *(6 marks)*

Sometimes it's easy to write loads more than you need, or too little, and to get the question wrong. So here is some guidance to help you with the time test from the previous page.

Question guidance

(a) (*2 marks*) The question requires that you write a brief answer. This means write two or three sentences. The stimulus gives you a clue to the term. If you refer to these three things, you are sure to have done enough for full marks.

(b) (*3 marks*) The question is asking you to explain how religious people can be guided by sources of authority. It says 'some of the ways' so you must give at least two – you do not have to list them all. You can give several ideas with an explanation, or you could explain just two in a bit more detail. If all you do is list, you will be unable to earn full marks because the question expects to see some explanation.

(c) (*3 marks*) The question is asking for your opinion on an attitude expressed in the statement. You may agree, disagree, be undecided or even have no strong opinions at all. It is important to remember that your opinion must be supported by reasons. A reason is different from an opinion because a reason can be supported with evidence. In the exam, you need to write an informed opinion using two or three reasons to be assured of full marks.

(d) (*4 marks*) Here, you need to write a clear and cohesive account to achieve full marks. Rambling answers can be overlong and cost you time in the exam, and they may not achieve full marks.

You need to write a descriptive account of a ceremony of commitment in one religious tradition. One approach is to think of the order of the ceremony from start to finish. Who is present, where does it take place, what is said and done, what symbols are used? You do not have to explain what happens. Don't worry if you can't remember everything, you can still achieve full marks for an answer if it is clearly and coherently written, including some of the main points.

(e) (*6 marks*) The full evaluation part always comes last in the question. It is worth spending a few moments structuring your answer. You will also need to include reference to at least one religious viewpoint, so it can be worth jotting down any ideas you have before you start. Remember, you are evaluating the attitude expressed in the statement NOT the topic in general.

In this question you are being asked to weigh up whether religion is more important to a believer than other aspects of life. You need to present reasons that agree and disagree with the attitude. It's a good idea to include examples to support your reasons. Work in this topic on the physical and spiritual dimensions of life, the roles and responsibilities people have and why some people commit to a religious tradition will be useful.

Remember, in evaluation it can also be useful to think wider than just the topic – you can probably think of ideas to argue against this statement that refer to life in general. If you use commonsense ideas effectively, you will be assured of a good mark. It's always a good idea to make sure you break your answer up into at least three clear paragraphs. You should finish by stating what your opinion of the statement is, with a reason or two.

Topic Six Religion and human rights

This topic is really about how religions view the law and life in a secular society. It considers the issue of human rights – what this term means and some examples of how those rights can be broken. Finally, it looks at the theme of protest and how specific people/organisations (religious and otherwise) have fought for human rights.

It is true to say that many religious people face difficulties within society because of their beliefs – their beliefs may clash with the laws and they may be victims of discrimination because of their beliefs (or showing what they believe). It is also true to say that an important principle of all religions is to fight for justice and oppose oppression. Keep in mind the basic religious teachings from pages 2–3 as you work through this topic – they are key.

What do we mean by human rights?

There are many descriptions and declarations of human rights. In a nutshell, they are the minimum rights every human being should be entitled to because they are human. They include basic rights and freedoms: right to life; to not be persecuted by others; to have a fair trial; to speak; and also the right to have food, shelter, education, healthcare and work.

The UN Declaration of Human Rights starts with the most fundamental: 'All humans are born free and equal in dignity and rights. They are endowed with reason and conscience and should act towards one another in a spirit of **brotherhood**.' Everything else comes from this really – laws are built on it, and our behaviour towards others should be governed by it.

Read the following situations. In each case, do you think there is a human right being denied or broken? If so, which right(s)?

Luke was beaten up because he kept making extremely racist comments.
Chris, aged 19, was told by the council they couldn't house him after his parents had thrown him out.
Sash didn't get into the school her parents chose because it was full – so they didn't send her to school.
Wayne was found guilty of murder and sentenced to death.

Task

1 Imagine you and 99 others have been stranded on a biosphere that is on Mars. There is no hope for anyone else from earth to get to you for many years. The biosphere allows for the production of food and recycling of all waste. It will sustain you all for as many years as you manage it properly (not overusing resources and maintaining systems so that they don't break down). You all realise very early on that a set of rules needs to be drawn up that everyone will live within. You are a mix of cultures and nationalities, with different expertise and experience. Your rules will only work if they are designed to protect a set of human rights. Your task is to decide what the rights of humans on Mars should be.

Now you have begun to think about human rights

The UN Declaration of Human Rights

Statements of rights have been written throughout history. Britain's first was probably the Magna Carta in 1215, which stated the ruler's commitment to his people. Setting out a code of rights is perhaps the first step in building law and legal systems.

2008 saw the sixtieth anniversary of the UN Declaration of Human Rights. It was written and then adopted by many countries in 1948, coming about partly because of the atrocities that countries fighting the Second World War had carried out. Although countries adopt this declaration, there is no binding requirement for them to keep it. These rights are in two distinct groups:

1 Civil and political rights.
2 Economic, social and cultural rights.

The UN claims that these are part of the way to build freedom, peace and justice in the world.

Let's take a look at some of these rights.

Everyone is:

- equal
- born free
- innocent until proven guilty.

Everyone should:

- be treated in the same way
- respect everyone else.

Everyone has the right to:

- legal protection
- a public trial
- asylum
- belong to a country
- marry
- own things and keep them
- free speech
- meet peacefully with others
- vote
- work
- rest
- an education
- basic rights – water, food, shelter, healthcare
- be an artist and enjoy the arts.

No one should be:

- tortured
- unfairly imprisoned.

No one may destroy the rights of others.

There must be laws to protect these rights.

Do you think that there are any rights missing? Or any that are wrong? Which do you think is the most important? Why? Do you think that everyone should always have rights? Is there ever a time when someone's rights should be reduced, or taken away?

Task

1 Look back to the four situations on page 77. Use the UN list of declared human rights to work out if any are being broken. If so, who by?
2 Read the newspaper headlines below. Why is each one a human rights issue?

Check out the UN website for more details of this topic: www.una.org.uk.

MORE THAN 1 MILLION CHILDREN UNDER 14 FORCED INTO PROSTITUTION EACH YEAR

NEW LAWS RUSHED IN TO STOP PROTESTORS

125 MILLION CHILDREN AGED 5–14 WORK FULL TIME TO SUPPORT THEIR FAMILIES

TSUNAMI VICTIMS DENIED HELP BY THEIR OWN GOVERNMENT

MAN CLAIMING ASYLUM TURNED AWAY AT AIRPORT

RACIST FIGHTS FOR ABSOLUTE FREEDOM OF SPEECH FOR HIMSELF

The Basics

1 What do we mean by human rights?
2 Explain how the UN Declaration of Human Rights came to be written.
3 List four human rights.
4 **The most important human right is for everyone to be free.** Do you agree? Give reasons for your answer, showing you have thought about more than one point of view. Refer to religious arguments in your answer.

Now you know something about the UN Declaration

The Human Rights Act 1998

The Human Rights Act (HRA) gave a legal standing in the UK to the fundamental rights and freedoms contained in the European Convention on Human Rights (ECHR). These are based on the UN Declaration. The HRA is supposed to ensure that people's human rights are protected and respected by public authorities. It makes it illegal for public authorities to act against a person's human rights. Everyone in the UK is protected by these rights.

The rights aren't absolute though – the government has the power to limit or control people's rights under certain conditions (in wartime, for instance). They also rely on people respecting each other and not behaving in a way that would go against other people's rights. You could go so far as to say that RESPECT is the key to everything, because respect for others leads to all those rights.

Being a religious citizen

What is a citizen?

Well, you are a citizen and so is your teacher and everyone else in your class. A citizen is a member of a country or nation. You are probably a British citizen; you are also a European citizen (because the UK is part of the European Union); you might have citizenship of another country, because some people have dual citizenship (usually because of having parents from different countries). Being a citizen brings rights within that country, but also responsibilities to respect and follow the rules of that country.

So, what is a religious citizen?

Well, it is simply someone who is a citizen, but has religious beliefs. Those beliefs should mean that they respect the law of the country in which they live or have citizenship. Generally speaking, British law is based on religious law. Both are based on RESPECT – that word keeps coming up, doesn't it? So religions would all agree with laws based around respect.

Sometimes the religious laws and secular laws don't match up – so what then?

Read the stories on the right, and try to work out what the people did. The answers are below.

David

My grandfather died suddenly. The doctors want to do a post-mortem. In my religion, we should not desecrate a body and should bury it whole. The post-mortem goes against both of those beliefs. Should we agree to the post-mortem or fight it?

Sarah

My grandfather was a Quaker and when the Second World War started, he was called up to fight. Quakers are pacifists – they don't believe in violence. The draft papers said he had to join the army – in wartime, of course a soldier has to fight. What do you think he did?

Mohan

I am a Sikh. My headmaster says my turban breaks school uniform rules. It is a part of my identity as a Sikh, and my religious duty to wear it. I have not been to school whilst banned from wearing it in school. I use the internet and books to help me study. What should I do?

David's family did not give permission, but the law can take that right away. His grandfather's body was subjected to a post-mortem exam before being released to the family for burial.

Sarah's grandfather claimed his right to be a conscientious objector. He was given a job in the UK for the war effort, but was subjected to much persecution and abuse, being called a traitor.

Mohan's case went to court and the House of Lords. It was ruled that wearing a turban is a religious duty, and schools have to respect that religious right.

Rights and organisations

This course is keen for you to have studied the work of some organisations in the field of human rights. You could be asked questions about how these organisations operate, why they exist and how they are supported. There is some information here, but you can check out the websites of all of the organisations to give your notes more detail, and yourself a better knowledge and understanding. We are going to look at the organisations that the specification lists – there are many more that you may wish to research.

Citizens Advice Bureaux (CAB)

The CAB was set up in 1939. The CAB 'values diversity, promotes equality and challenges discrimination' – truly a human rights organisation for the UK. It is a British charity-based organisation that helps people to resolve legal, financial and other problems. It doesn't solve the problems; rather it gives free information and advice to people so that they can sort out their problems. There are over 420 CAB centres in the UK, which are staffed almost entirely by volunteers – some 20,000 of them. In a year, those centres and volunteers will help in over 5.5 million issues for almost 2 million people – that is 1 in 30 of the British population.

The money to run all this comes from many sources – local authorities, lottery grants, companies and individuals, for example.

So, how does the CAB help people?

Well, CAB volunteers speak with people and give advice, or point them in the direction of others who can help. They write letters for people, make phone calls and can help prepare a case for court. Advice is English and Welsh and other community languages – showing the diversity of Britain today. The CAB also works to influence policy makers – to make society fairer in law and practice. It runs a number of campaigns, such as End Child Poverty and Right to Justice.

Find out more about the work and importance of the CAB at: www.citizensadvice.org.uk.

ChildLine

ChildLine is the UK's 24 hour free and confidential telephone helpline for children and young people below age 19. ChildLine aims to be someone to turn to for every young person whenever they feel unsafe or unhappy so they can be protected, comforted and helped to make their lives better. By phoning 0800 1111 young callers can talk about any problem with a trained volunteer counsellor. ChildLine listens to what a young person thinks and feels about whatever is troubling them and helps them find a way forward that keeps them safe and feels right for them. ChildLine doesn't do things that young callers can do for themselves because it wants children to grow in confidence to help themselves and others. What a young person tells ChildLine stays private but if they are in a life threatening situation, and unable or unwilling to seek emergency help for themselves, then ChildLine will contact the police or ambulance service.

In February 2006 ChildLine joined the National Society for Prevention of Cruelty to Children. NSPCC has raised money to help ChildLine keep its promise to answer every child's call and has launched the Child's Voice Appeal with the slogan, 'Let no cry go unheard.'

Visit www.childline.org.uk.

Samaritans

Samaritans was set up by Chad Varah in 1953. He was a Church of England vicar whose parish was in London. He met many people in his time as a vicar who he wanted to be able to help, but felt he could not. He set up a counselling service, with him doing the counselling and volunteers chatting and serving tea, and so on. He soon realised that he had created a befriending service whereby his volunteers listened and gave their undivided attention without making judgements on what they heard. This helped because it gave people in emotional distress the time and space to work out their thoughts and issues.

Today, Samaritans handles over 5 million contacts a year, half of which are silent – the person on the other end of the phone is too distressed even to be able to speak. About 90 per cent of these contacts are by phone. More men than women use the service. The service is offered by 16,534 trained volunteers and is entirely dependent on voluntary support. More women than men volunteer for Samaritans providing over 2 million hours of emotional support a year.

Samaritans doesn't offer advice, but by encouraging people who contact them to talk about their feelings they are able to help them explore all the options they have. Samaritans believes that given the time and space to work problems or difficulties through in confidence, people can find an inner strength and perspective, which lets them find their own way forward.

You can contact Samaritans by phone, email, SMS, letter or face to face by visiting one of their 202 branches.

Find out more about Samaritans on their website: www.samaritans.org

Amnesty International

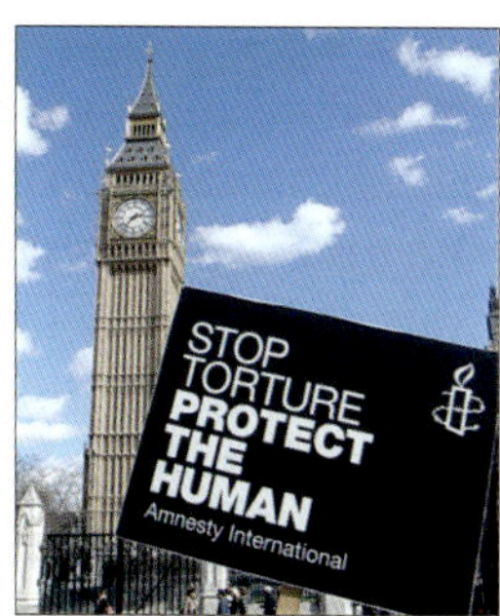

Amnesty International is one of the world's most well-known human rights organisations. It was set up in 1961, after a campaign by Peter Benenson had called for protest against those people who were imprisoned because of their political or religious beliefs. Today, over 2.2 million members make up this organisation, and many others get involved in its work. Amnesty's stated purpose is to 'protect individuals wherever justice, fairness and truth are denied'.

Amnesty uses the UN Declaration of Human Rights as its basis, and will protest and campaign whenever those rights are being abused. It commissions reports and research that can be used to pressure governments into action. It sets up protests on many issues – current campaigns include 'Stop Violence Against Women', 'Terrorism and Security', and 'Human Rights in China'. Perhaps Amnesty is most famous for its work with prisoners of conscience and those on death row. For prisoners of conscience, it is simply about their right to free speech, or to believe what they want to believe. For those on death row, many have been unfairly sentenced to death.

Find out more about Amnesty's work today and, at the same time, learn about some of the human rights abuses going on in the world. This will give you a lot of information to use in the exam. Check out the website: www.amnesty.org.uk.

Task

For each of the organisations above and on page 80, carry out some research. Find out:

- how the organisation came about
- how the organisation operates
- what the organisation does
- why each can be considered an organisation working for human rights.

Put your findings together in a series of fact sheets – one for each organisation.

Fighting for rights

You have just learned about four organisations that fight for the rights of different groups of people and individuals. We can call these groups **pressure groups**, because they try to put pressure on society and on governments and businesses to make change happen. For this course, you need to know about the work of some pressure groups. You will meet some more later in the topic.

Pressure groups are all engaged in forms of protest. They don't agree with something that is happening, and make that disagreement publicly known. The publicity could be local, national or international, but it is intended to cause pressure that will lead to change. You need to learn about protest for this course.

Task

1 Read the following statements.
   a Why is each person protesting?
   b What are they protesting about?

In my religion, we have to fight for those who are being persecuted – it is my religious duty.
Callum

I just think it is morally wrong to experiment on animals, so I joined the protest.
Sasha

The only way to get things changed is to show that enough people don't agree – so I am adding my voice to all the others to save the hospital.
Kym

I protested at the airport because the noise and pollution for even more planes would ruin my life.
Benji

I have to stand up for political prisoners because they can't do it for themselves – I feel morally obliged to.
Ailsa

2 There will be many more reasons why people protest. Can you think of reasons why you might protest?

Examiner's Tip

Be careful – question 2 is asking you *why* people use this form of action, not *what* are they protesting about. In the exam, it is easy to do the latter when the question wants the former.

So how do people protest? Check out the graffiti and work out some of the different methods of protest. Can you think of other ways? Do you think some would be more effective than others? What and why?

Why a graffiti wall? Well, graffiti is actually one form of protest – you write what you disagree with on the wall. The protest, though, is meant to block something – abuse of rights, closures happening, new building, and so on. So, if you try to remember the wall with the ideas, you might remember one of the main aims of protest as well.

Research Task

Find out about the following people. They all protested. Find out how they protested and why they protested in that manner, as well as what they were trying to achieve.

- Thich Quang Duc (1963).
- Abas Amini (2003).
- Martin Luther King, Jr (1955).
- Emily Wilding Davison (1913).

Now you know more about protest

Religion and protest

It is important that you know if religions protest, and if so, how and why they do it.

Buddhism 

Do Buddhists protest?

Yes. During the Vietnam War, Buddhists protested. One famous protest photograph shows a monk who set fire to himself so that he would burn to death.

Tibetan Buddhists have protested against what they see as the occupation of Tibet by China for many years.

Why do Buddhists protest?

Protesting against injustice can be seen as the positive side of the precept to 'not harm others'. It could also be judged as 'right speech' and 'right action' (two parts of the Noble Eightfold Path) because Buddhists are speaking out or acting against injustice. Since compassion is central to Buddhism, trying to make change happen to improve things for other people is good.

How do Buddhists protest?

The Dalai Lama speaks only of non-violence – only when there is an atmosphere of mutual respect, will there be peace and harmony. The Buddhist beliefs above also point Buddhists towards non-violent protest.

Having said this, the Buddhist monk who burnt himself to death used a violent form of protest, even though it was against himself.

Find out more about Thich Quang Duc's protest.

Christianity ✝

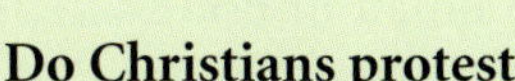

Do Christians protest?

Yes, for example Martin Luther King and the American black Civil Rights Movement.

Christians are taught to fight injustice. The Gospel of Luke shows Jesus helping non-Jews and outcasts from society.

Why do Christians protest?

The Bible states that everyone is equal because God made us all. So, we should treat others as equals and make sure everyone has equal rights – this means protecting **minority groups**.

How do Christians protest?

Martin Luther King protested non-violently through marches, demonstrations and sit-ins, believing that violence did not solve problems in the long term. Jesus said 'Blessed are the peacemakers'. He also told Christians to turn the other cheek in the face of violence and to love their enemies.

Some Christians believe that sometimes violence is necessary; without it change cannot be forced and many people suffer for much longer. God gave us freedom of will and choice. We have to use both responsibly, but, ultimately, it is up to each of us to decide how to react.

Find out how far Dietrich Bonhoeffer was prepared to go in his fight for rights.

Hinduism 🕉

Do Hindus protest?

Yes. Mahatma Gandhi led protest against British rule in India in the early twentieth century. He had already protested against apartheid in South Africa, and went on to protest for equal rights for all castes in India. As a committed Hindu, this was as much a religious act as anything else.

Why do Hindus protest?

The virtues of shelter for and service to others should encourage any Hindu to protest where they see injustice. Compassion and tolerance should help them to see the injustice in the first place and want to do something to change it.

How do Hindus protest?

Gandhi believed only in non-violent protest, because that was the only correct way to achieve the goal. The Arya Samaj was set up to try to break down caste barriers through making untouchables a part of their society, and providing opportunities for them, in other words, treating them as equals. Their work is achieved through political pressure and non-violent means. All Hindus should follow ahimsa – non-violence.

Find out how Gandhi fought for human rights.

Islam ☪

Do Muslims protest?

Yes, they do protest. In recent history, it has been a common news story that Muslims are protesting, for example, in relation to events in Iraq or in Palestinian lands. You have probably seen examples for yourself.

Why do Muslims protest?

Muslims have a duty to fellow Muslims to support them, and this can mean protest. In the UK, we have seen Muslim-organised protests, for example, against racism and Islamophobia, and against the war in Iraq. Freedom of conscience and religion is part of the Islamic Declaration of Human Rights and protected for non-Muslims in Muslim countries, so where that is contravened Muslims should protest.

How do Muslims protest?

Islam means 'peace'. Muhammad (pbuh) said that all Muslims should be peaceful in their behaviour, and violence is forbidden except in self-defence. Islam allows anyone to protest against anything that they feel is unfair or don't accept. The protest should not put someone's life at risk though. Violence is always a last resort, but there is an acceptance that, if all else fails, violence can be used. Also, Muslims are expected to hit back when struck, as stated in the Qur'an. This means that violent harassment, for example, could be repaid with violence. As it is a Muslim's duty to fight oppression, we sometimes see violence in the name of Islam. One example was the Black Muslim Movement and Malcolm X, who fought against racist violence in the USA. Another is the Palestinian struggle in Israel, where Palestinians use suicide bombings to try to force change.

Find out about Ilgar Ibrahimoglu and his fight for human rights.

Judaism

Do Jews protest?

Yes. One Jewish tradition is to protest against injustice, and to work to make the world a better place. This is because they believe G-d put them on earth as stewards, and stewardship is over people and the world. There is a duty to support others, including through protest, because we are all made in G-d's image. The books of the Neviim give many stories of prophets who protested long and loud about the behaviour of nations, groups and individuals. It is a part of Jewish history.

Why do Jews protest?

They remember that Jews have been persecuted many times in history. Part of preventing that from happening again is to voice protest. They also have an obligation to better life for humanity and, at times, protest is for this reason.

How do Jews protest?

You may have seen Jewish protest marches and demonstrations on TV – against anti-Semitism, against the events in Israel, occupation and resettlement. These protests are non-violent. The organisation Jews for Global Justice (www.SocialAction.com) uses direct action and civil disobedience in its protest. Civil disobedience is when you refuse to comply with laws as a form of protest.

Find out about Yelena Bonner and her human rights work.

The Basics

1 For the religion(s) you are studying, give two examples of protest by that religion.
2 What values make members of your chosen religion protest? Use the basic teachings from pages 2–3 to help you.
3 In what ways might the members of your chosen religion protest?
4 Do they agree with non-violent protest? Explain your answer, using the basic teachings from pages 2–3.
5 **Protesting peacefully does nothing but give more time to the injustice you are protesting about.**
   a Give three reasons to agree, and explain them.
   b Give three reasons to disagree, and explain them.
   Make sure at least two of your reasons are linked to religious ideas.

Sikhism

Do Sikhs protest?

For Sikhs, it is important that people are not persecuted for their beliefs. Where they see this happening, they should act, which can involve protest. One of the key values for Sikhs is sewa – service to others. This should motivate them to protest where they see injustice. In early 2005, the British press reported Sikhs protesting against a theatre production that they said was unfair to their religion. Sikhs have also protested for many years in a bid to have a homeland country in the area that is the Punjab of India.

Why do Sikhs protest?

They have a duty to protect and defend those who are being persecuted. This leads to Sikhs lending their voice to protest in these matters. They also protest when they feel there is a moral wrong happening that affects their own religion, for example Sikhs protested about 'Jerry Springer – The Opera' because of its portrayal of a Sikh.

How do Sikhs protest?

Since one aim of Sikhism is not to harm others, protest will usually be peaceful. However, Sikhism is a warrior religion and some of its symbols are swords. This shows the willingness to physically fight for justice and equality that exists in Sikh values.

Find out about the work and life of Jaswant Singh Khalra.

Now you know about religion and protest

Protests and organisations

Individuals and groups can and do protest. You have already seen this. Religions support protest, especially where rights are violated. However, the real power of protest is often in it being coordinated and prolonged. This is where organisations come in.

If a whole group of people is being discriminated against or persecuted, it is unlikely that one person alone can make change happen. There are many small groups in society; however, these should still have an equality of life and the same rights as everyone else. Yet, these groups are often victims of discrimination. We call them **minority groups**, and their rights **minority rights**. It is the pressure groups who are often most effective in fighting for these people.

For the exam, you need to know about some pressure groups. Pressure groups are organisations set up to fight a cause – pressurising the government, society or business to change. Pressure groups are usually funded through charity, not the government, because they are often fighting the government.

What do you think organisations can do better than individuals and small groups?

- Organisations can be big – Amnesty International has over 2 million members.
- Their size gives them power – 2 million people writing to the prime minister has a bigger impact than twenty.
- Organisations have more money from memberships and fundraising – this can fund research and legal proceedings, amongst other things.
- The money and their size gains the organisation more publicity – which means more airtime for their protest.

Any more reasons?

The organisations in this book have proven track records of success in human rights – whether it be for adults or children, on political or religious grounds, whatever their cause. Their success tells us that the organisations are needed, but also that they do make change happen.

Do you think religious believers should support pressure groups? Explain why?

Stevie: So, you are joining Amnesty?

Wayne: Yes. I think their rights work is important. It helps a lot of people.

Stevie: What if they did a violent protest? Would you still support them?

Wayne: I don't believe in violence, but Amnesty isn't about that. Some people might be though – I wouldn't take part in that kind of protest. Always peaceful, you know.

Stevie: So, what is the point of it anyway?

Wayne: You get to have your say – a big organisation has lots of clout really. I can't get things changed on my own. This way I can help to make a change for the better in the world.

Stevie: What if what they were arguing for was against your beliefs?

Wayne: Well, I wouldn't support them – just like you wouldn't. It is all about what you agree and disagree with, and how strongly you feel. If I feel very strongly about something, I have to do something – joining Amnesty is just that. Can't just sit and moan at the telly!

Greenpeace

Greenpeace (www.greenpeace.org.uk) began in 1971, when a small boat of volunteers and journalists sailed into Amchitka to provide proof that the US government was involved in secret underground nuclear testing. Its aim was to expose this activity. Today, Greenpeace has almost 3 million supporters in the UK alone who help fund its work.

Greenpeace believes that the earth is in a fragile state and needs people to speak for it – to protect and defend it. Greenpeace tries to be that voice.

It campaigns non-violently in many specific actions – for example, against climate change, to protect ancient forests, to stop whaling and to encourage sustainable trade. Campaigns might include public demonstrations, publicising research, and political lobbying. Many Greenpeace campaigns are very high profile.

Abortion Rights

Abortion is legal in the UK under set circumstances. However, many believe it is not available in a way that helps women – rather the system makes a very difficult situation and decision even more difficult.

Abortion Rights (www.abortionrights.org.uk) is an organisation that was formed by the merger of the National Abortion Campaign and the Abortion Law Reform Association in 2003. It believes that every woman has the right to decide what happens to her body, including having an abortion. It also believes that women should be able to make that decision in supportive surroundings, and that it should be an NHS-funded service.

It campaigns for law reform, especially aimed at making sure the law works, for example, stopping doctors from blocking abortion requests. It campaigns through petitions, publications and political lobbying.

Society for the Protection of the Unborn Child (SPUC)

SPUC (www.spuc.org.uk) was set up in 1966 to try to fight against the bill that was to become the Abortion Act 1967. It was the first pro-life organisation in the world. SPUC's aim is to defend human life from conception to natural death, and it is most famous for its work around abortion. It takes as its guiding principle the UN Declaration Right that states that children need special protection. SPUC aims to defend and assist the life and welfare of mothers.

SPUC is a charity and has to fundraise to do its work. This work includes political lobbying, producing educational materials and silent vigils.

Task

1. Check the newspapers to find out about current human rights issues. The exam could ask you about a current issue – what is happening, and how it is being fought.
2. Check out the following organisations:
   - World Wildlife Fund
   - Stonewall
   - Fawcett Society
   - Shelter
   - Rethink.

   a. What are they fighting for?
   b. How do they fight?
   c. What are the rights involved in their fight?
   d. How successful have they been in their campaigns?

Mind

Mind (www.mind.org.uk) is a charity that fights for the rights of those who suffer from mental illness. Mind wants to make it possible for people who experience mental distress to live full lives and play their full part in society. It is the leading mental health charity in the UK.

Mind's work includes acting as an advocate for the mentally ill. They challenge discrimination of, and promote inclusion for, mentally ill people. They work to influence laws so that institutional discrimination is reduced. They fight for better quality services for the mentally ill, and to gain equal rights for them.

For mentally ill people and their families, Mind is a very important organisation because of the help and support it gives. Its work is crucial in our society today.

The Howard League for Penal Reform

The Howard League for Penal Reform (www.howardleague.org) was named after John Howard, one of the first prison reformers who lived in the nineteenth century. It was set up in 1921 after two organisations merged – the Howard Association and the Penal Reform League.

The League doesn't believe that criminals should not be punished, but it does fight to make prison conditions better. This will then enable real work to take place with prisoners to help them to reform and so return to society able to fit in and respect the law.

The League runs campaigns about different issues that it sees as key – such as child prisoners and real work opportunities in prisons. It wants to make prisons make a difference, whilst accepting there is something redeemable about everyone – given the right support and opportunities.

The Basics

1. For each of the organisations listed:
   - a Who are they?
   - b What do they do?
   - c Which human right(s) are their protests based on?
   - d Find out about one of their campaigns.
2. Find out about a local/regional pressure group. Find out the details asked for in question 1 above. Present the information as a poster.

Last words

You could be asked questions about local and regional rights issues, and about the work of rights activists. You met some names earlier in the topic for the activists, and can just check the web for new names regularly. You now have several examples of organisations that support people with rights issues, and that fight for change.

However, it is impossible for the issues mentioned in this book to remain current – you may be reading it months after it was written, perhaps even years – and times change! It is also impossible for the authors of this book to give issues local to you (unless you live in North Manchester)! So, keep a good eye on the news – get your own examples, keep a scrapbook, decide how you feel about the issues. Use the UN Declaration of Human Rights to help you decide whether or not something is a rights issue and then follow its progress. You might even get involved – now there is real citizenship for you!

Now you know about pressure groups

Exam tips – building your technique

Let's start with a bunch of questions, and use them for each task on this page.

1 Explain what is meant by human rights.
2 Explain what is meant by protest.
3 Why do people join pressure groups?
4 In your own words, describe the work of an individual who has fought for human rights.
5 Explain religious attitudes to protest. Use beliefs and teachings in your answer.
6 In your opinion, which are the most important human rights and why?

Getting to an F grade

Actually, it is quite easy to make an F grade. Your teacher must have told you that you should try to answer every question. They are right – you can't lose any marks for getting anything wrong.

So, you need to be able to give one correct answer to every question or, if you can, a couple of correct answers.

Try to give one answer to each of the questions. Remember it has to be relevant and correct to get the mark.

So, if you did that all through the paper, you'd walk an F grade. But you don't just want that, do you? So let's look at building on that F, and getting the C.

Getting to a C grade

If you just had to get 1 mark per question to get an F, now you'll have to get 2 marks to get a C. You will have to give two different and correct ideas in each answer.

Boys are really good at writing the first thing that comes into their head, and then moving on to the next question. As examiners, the authors of this book see this all the time – and your teacher will back this up. So, get into the habit of giving two answers. Crack that habit, and then you'll be ready to make your move on the highest grades.

If the topics on the paper are split into five parts (as AQA recommends to principal examiners), 2 marks for every part means you'll accumulate about 40 marks across the paper. The paper is out of 72, so this will be enough for a C grade, and could well be enough for a B.

Okay, try to give two answers to each of the questions. It's okay to reuse the answers you used earlier – but you'll feel even cleverer if you can come up with two new ones!

Getting to an A grade

The thing is, to get an A grade, you can't just give relevant answers. You have to explain yourself. We're talking about showing that you can develop ideas, that you can evaluate comments and make judgements. They are quite tough skills. However, you can train yourself to do a bit more with your answer, and so improve it. If you can grab 3 of every 4 marks available, you *will* get that A grade.

Here's the technique: when you have given your two answers (for the C grade – remember), explain one of them by developing the point and providing an example to show what you mean. Or explain both of the points.

You can do this for any of the topics, and you need to really, so that you get good practice using the techniques. Lots of practice means you will do it without even thinking about what you are doing – it becomes the way you write. Now that isn't just good for this subject – it helps to build marks in all of your subjects.

Appendix I

Revision outline

This is a revision guide. It follows the outline of topics in the specification.

Use the guide as a checklist of what you know, and what you have still got to get to grips with. You could even use it as a last-minute check before you go into the exam. When you have finished all your revision, you should be able to recognise each word. Each phrase should trigger a whole lot of ideas in your head – definitions, examples and explanations. When it does, you are ready.

TOPIC	**WORDS TO LEARN**	**SUBJECTS WITHIN TOPIC – DO YOU KNOW…?**
ONE: RELIGION AND RELATIONSHIPS	Commitment Contract Covenant Responsibility Heterosexuality Homosexuality Age of consent Sex before marriage Adultery Contraception Vows Parenting Divorce	• How the key terms – commitment, contract, covenant and responsibility – apply to relationships • Religious attitudes to sex – heterosexuality/homosexuality • Religious attitudes to the age of consent • Religious attitudes to sex before marriage • Religious attitudes to adultery • Religious attitudes to contraception • Why people marry • About religious marriage ceremonies • Attitudes to marriage alternatives, e.g. civil partnerships, cohabitation • Religious attitudes to parental involvement in the choice of a marriage partner for their children • Attitudes to mixed race and faith marriages • Why people have children • Religious attitudes to parenting as a role • Roles within the family • Why people get divorced • Religious attitudes to divorce • Society's attitude to all of the above
TWO: RELIGION, SPORT AND LEISURE	Leisure Relaxation Morality in sport Performance-enhancing drugs Chaplain Belonging Inspiration Sponsorship Gambling Devotion Sabbath/Shabbat Prejudice	• What counts as leisure and why do we have it • The benefits of leisure activities • Attitudes to winning at all costs • Attitudes to the use of performance-enhancing drugs • Attitudes to money in sports • How fans show their devotion to their team • Whether we can call sport a religion • The issues on which sport and religion clash, e.g. Sabbath/Shabbat observance • Where sportsmen get their ability from – nature, nurture, God? • Attitudes to prejudice within sport, e.g. race, gender, disability • Religious attitudes to all of the above

TOPIC	WORDS TO LEARN	SUBJECTS WITHIN TOPIC – DO YOU KNOW...?
THREE: RELIGION AND WORK	Work Service Sewa Vocation Career Business Enterprise Tithing Responsibility Minimum wage Trade union Sabbath/Shabbat Voluntary work Unemployment	• Why people work • Why people see work as service/sewa • About a believer who regarded work as a vocation • What are acceptable forms of earning money • What are unacceptable forms of earning money – and why • Attitudes to taxation and tithing • About the rights and responsibilities of employees/employers • Why people do voluntary work with examples • About a religious organisation that is based on voluntary work • Why there is unemployment • The problems caused by being unemployed • About support mechanisms for the unemployed • Religious attitudes to all of the above
FOUR: RELIGION AND MULTICULTURAL SOCIETY	Tolerance Respect Diversity Multiculturalism Political correctness Politics Segregation Blasphemy laws Asylum seeker Immigration Emigration Integration Faith community Festival Celebration	• How the key terms of tolerance, respect, diversity, multiculturalism, and political correctness apply • How religion shapes politics • How religion and politics clash • The advantages of being in a multicultural society • The disadvantages of being in a multicultural society • What it means to have a State religion • Why there are blasphemy laws, and how they are enforced • How freedom of choice affects the religion a person follows, and their behaviour • How the UK has a changing population • How faith communities have an influence on society • Major religious festivals – how and why they are celebrated

TOPIC	WORDS TO LEARN	SUBJECTS WITHIN TOPIC – DO YOU KNOW...?
FIVE: RELIGION AND IDENTITY	Humanity Spirituality Purpose Self-worth/self-esteem Identity Commitment Leadership Brotherhood Custom Symbolism Healthy living Morality Conscience	• What it means to be human • What makes us each individual • What the purpose and meaning of life is • How we gain our sense of self-worth/self-esteem • How people join faith communities • Roles within faith communities, e.g. leadership, brotherhood • How people show their belonging to faith communities through dress and tradition/custom • Religious attitudes to healthy living • How religious people make moral decisions, e.g. using holy books, conscience, leaders, etc. • How religious believers belong to several different groups, often diverse and clashing
SIX: RELIGION AND HUMAN RIGHTS	Human rights Responsibility Citizenship United Nations Pressure group Protest Minority rights	• Religious attitudes to the law • Religious attitudes to human rights • What we mean by human rights • The role of the UN in protecting human rights • The role of government in protecting human rights • Organisations that help the abused, e.g. the CAB, ChildLine, Samaritans • About local and national human rights issues • How pressure groups operate with examples • Why people support pressure groups • How and why people protest • Why religious people support non-religious organisations • About some individuals and religious groups who have supported human rights

Appendix II

Sample Paper

What a question paper looks like

You will be given a question paper and an answer booklet in the examination.

Do I really need to read the cover? It's always the same isn't it?

Well, no, they aren't all the same, and it is easy in a stressful situation to mix up what you are meant to do. Probably your teacher will have told you a million times what you have to do in the exam, but you can still forget. It is still a good idea to just check through the cover – it is like a calming exercise that helps if you are nervous. It also reassures you that you do know what you are doing.

The cover will remind you:

- how long the exam lasts – so plan and use your time well. Reassess after each full question answered – you might have gained or lost some time. Don't spend too much time on one question, but don't rush yourself either. You start with four questions to answer in 90 minutes – about 22 minutes a question.
- that you get a choice of any four of the six questions on offer. If you answer them all, you'll be given marks for the best four, but it might not be the best use of your time. Some people find they have lots of time left when they have finished what they should do, so they do extra questions to pass the time!
- that you can choose one or two religions for each question. If you have studied two religions, then it is a good idea to answer every question that asks for religious attitudes as if it was the same question twice, once for each religion. Your answer will be much clearer, and so easier to mark.
- to use blue or black ink/pen. This makes your paper easier to read and mark. This is especially important when exam papers are going to be marked online. You need your writing to be clear and bold, so the examiner doesn't have to struggle to read it.
- that you should do any notes or practice work on either your answer booklet, or on extra paper. Sometimes, people write correct things that they then don't put into their real answer. If you hand in all your working out and notes, the examiner can credit you for anything you missed out. They are obliged to read it all. In your answer booklet, write on the lines only – don't go into the margins or above/below the box. The online mark reader (OMR) system that scans your booklet into the computer for the examiner to mark online isn't designed to pick up anything outside of the writing area – it might cost you marks.

So much for the cover, what about the inside?

There will be six questions and the chances are that each one will have a picture or some writing to start with. The pictures are meant to stimulate your brain and start you thinking. In other words, they are meant to help you by triggering the relevant ideas for that question.

In this sample paper, the marks in the questions are split 2/3/4/3/6. There has to be a 3 and a 6-mark evaluative, but the other 9 marks could be split up in a different way – it could be 1/2/6, 1/3/5 or 4/5, for example. So be prepared (through the practice in this book) for this.

There are six questions. You have to answer four. If you answer more, your best four will be used to work out your grade.

Answer any **four** questions

Each question is worth **18 marks**

9 marks for knowledge-type questions. 9 marks for 'Do you agree?'-type questions.

1. Religion and relationships

The stimulus is meant to be a help in answering questions.

(1.1) What is meant by the term 'sexuality'? *(2 marks)*

You need to make two points, or explain one to get full marks. Examples are good here.

(1.2) 'Religious people should not be in a gay relationship.'

What do you think? Explain your answer. *(3 marks)*

For this kind of evaluation, you can give one side or two sides.

(1.3) Explain religious attitudes to sex before marriage. Refer to beliefs and teachings in your answer. *(4 marks)*

One or two religions – both ways are okay.

(1.4) Explain why many religious couples see marriage as a covenant. *(3 marks)*

Don't just list points, explain them.

Give at least two reasons.

(1.5) 'Marriage ceremonies should always take place in a religious building.'

Do you agree? Give reasons for your answer, showing you have thought about more than one point of view. Refer to religious arguments in your answer. *(6 marks)*

DREARER – remember?

Learn the DREARER formula for good evaluative responses:

Disagree with the statement.
Reasons why you disagree.
Explanations of some of those reasons.
Agree with the statement.
Reasons why you agree.
Explanations of some of those reasons.
Religious argument must be in there.

Don't get phased – it isn't that hard to get 4 or more marks for these – just follow the formula.

2. Religion, sport and leisure

(2.1) What is meant by the term 'leisure'? (*2 marks*)

How is it similar? How is it different?

(2.2) 'Sport can be said to be like a religion.'

What do you think? Explain your opinion. (*3 marks*)

(2.3) Explain religious attitudes to the use of performance-enhancing drugs. Refer to beliefs and teachings in your answer. (*4 marks*)

Don't talk about anything but benefits. Negative aspects of leisure time would get no marks here.

(2.4) Explain the benefits of leisure time. (*3 marks*)

(2.5) 'Professional sports people are paid too much money.'

Do you agree? Give reasons for your answer, showing you have thought about more than one point of view. Refer to religious arguments in your answer. (*6 marks*)

These questions are often most easily answered by starting with 'It depends…' By writing like this, you create lots of pathways for your answer to follow.

3. Religion and work

(3.1) What is meant by the term 'minimum wage'? *(2 marks)*

(3.2) 'Religious people should give 10 per cent of their wages to charity.'
What do you think? Explain your opinion. *(3 marks)*

(3.3) Explain religious attitudes to voluntary work. Refer to beliefs and teachings in your answer. *(4 marks)*

Don't write about jobs, just write about the things we *volunteer* for, i.e. not paid.

(3.4) Explain the problems caused by unemployment. *(3 marks)*

You could answer for the individual or for society here.

(3.5) 'Working for God is the most important aspect of work.'
Do you agree? Give reasons for your answer, showing you have thought about more than one point of view. Refer to religious arguments in your answer. *(6 marks)*

4. Religion and multicultural society

(4.1) What is meant by 'blasphemy'? *(2 marks)*

Say what it means and give an example for the 2 marks.

(4.2) 'Religion should not try to influence how a country is run.'

What do you think? Explain your opinion. *(3 marks)*

(4.3) Explain religious attitudes to living in a multicultural society. Refer to beliefs and teachings in your answer. *(4 marks)*

This question is simply about accepting people with different views from yours.

(4.4) Explain why religious believers celebrate religious festivals. *(3 marks)*

Key word here, don't bother naming festivals just say why they are celebrated.

(4.5) 'Having many religions in one country just confuses everyone.'

Do you agree? Give reasons for your answer, showing you have thought about more than one point of view. Refer to religious arguments in your answer. *(6 marks)*

5. Religion and identity

(5.1) What is meant by the term 'conscience'? *(2 marks)*

(5.2) 'Sacred writings are the most important source of right and wrong.'

What do think? Explain your opinion. *(3 marks)*

Don't waste time by describing more than one.

(5.3) Describe **one** religious ceremony of commitment you have studied. *(4 marks)*

(5.4) Explain why religious believers think humans are special. *(3 marks)*

(5.5) 'There is no such thing as a spiritual dimension.'

Do you agree? Give reasons for your answer, showing you have thought about more than one point of view. Refer to religious arguments in your answer. *(6 marks)*

6. Religion and human rights

(6.1) What is meant by the term 'human rights'? *(2 marks)*

(6.2) 'Religious people should fight for the rights of every minority group.'

What do you think? Explain your opinion. *(3 marks)*

Focus on this in your answer.

(6.3) Explain religious attitudes to protest. Refer to beliefs and teachings in your answer. *(4 marks)*

Whether it is right or wrong not when they should protest.

(6.4) Explain why religious believers join pressure groups. *(3 marks)*

(6.5) 'The most important human right is freedom to believe in a religion.'

Do you agree? Give reasons for your answer, showing you have thought about more than one point of view. Refer to religious arguments in your answer. *(6 marks)*

Glossary

Adultery to have an affair (sex with someone other than your husband/wife)

Age of consent the age at which a person is considered old enough to be able to decide to have sex, according to the law

Amateur status a sport played as a hobby, rather than at a professional level

Asylum seeker a person seeking safety in another country for political, religious or social reasons

Blasphemy laws the laws regarding rude or disrespectful words/actions to God or something sacred

Brotherhood friendship or companionship between people with something in common

Business a trade; the act of buying and selling goods or services

Career a person's chosen job

Chastity keeping oneself sexually pure, e.g. waiting until marriage before having sex

Celibacy not having sexual relations

Citizen a person belonging to a city or a country

Civil partnership the legal union of two people of the same sex (civil marriage)

Commitment the act of making a promise or pledge

Conscience a voice inside us telling us what is right; The 'voice of God'

Contraception precautions taken to prevent pregnancy and to protect against sexually transmitted infections (STIs)

Contract a binding, formal agreement between two sides

Covenant an agreement based on promises between two sides; often linked to religion, so includes an agreement before and with God

Culture the beliefs and traditions of a particular people

Devotion great love or loyalty, particularly in terms of religion

Discretionary leave people who have been refused asylum but are allowed to remain in the country where they applied for asylum on compassionate or exceptional grounds, e.g. unaccompanied asylum-seeking children

Discrimination acting on one's prejudice

Diversity the mix of people and cultures in a society

Divorce the legal ending of a marriage

Emigration to leave a country to settle, live and work in another

Employee/employer paid worker/person who employs the worker

Enterprise a person's creative spirit/business activity; to undertake a project

Fair competition where all compete under the same conditions

Faith community a group of people who are part of a particular religion

Family parents and children

Festival celebration of a key event within a religion; for this course: Wesak; Christmas; Divali; Id-ul-Fitr; Pesach; and Baisakhi

Gambling to bet on a race, or the outcome of an event, with money

Healthy living a mixture of good diet, exercise and looking after body and mind

Heterosexuality being physically attracted to the opposite sex

Homosexuality being physically attracted to the same sex

Human rights the basic rights and freedoms of human beings

Humanitarian protection the UK government believes that if refugees return to their country, their human rights will be infringed in an unacceptable way. Therefore, they are given rights to remain and, after five years, may be granted indefinite leave if they still need protection.

Identity how a person defines themselves; to recognise a person as being who or what they are. This could be different in various situations.

Immigration the act of coming into a country to live permanently

Integration to bring people of different faiths and cultures together

Interdependence people who are reliant on one another

Law the legal system in a country that people must live by

Leisure spare time when not at work

Lesser of two evils where there are two bad choices/options, one is not quite as bad as the other, so it is accepted

Marriage the legal joining of two people as husband and wife

Minimum wage the lowest hourly rate an employee can be paid by law

Minority group a small group of people that differs from the majority in some way, e.g. in language, nationality, religion or culture

Minority rights the rights of people who are in groups of small numbers – often targeted by groups with larger numbers

Multiculturalism the belief of racial, cultural and ethnic harmony in a country

Multiple identities the idea that each of us has to fit into many different groups, and we create a persona for each of those – so our role at home is different to that at school; our role as a member of a village differs from that as a UK citizen, and so on

Necessary evil a bad option that must be taken for a good purpose/intention

Parenting the act of being a good mother or father

Performance-enhancing drugs used in sport to improve performance and enhance chances of winning – often steroids

Political correctness language, ideas and policies that seek to reduce offence to gender, race, sexuality, disability, age or other named groups

Prejudice prejudging someone based on an idea or opinion formed before getting to know them, often a stereotypical and negative idea

Pressure group an organised group that campaigns for change on set issues, including trying to influence public policy on those issues

Professionalism to do a full-time job and be paid for it, not as an amateur

Protest an action to show that you disagree with something

Racism prejudice against someone of a different race or culture

Refugee someone who has an asylum application agreed and who is recognised as a refugee under the UN 1951 Convention of Refugees and can remain in the country where they applied for asylum

Respect politeness and consideration for others

Responsibility a duty; a legal or moral obligation; something we have to do

Sabbath/Shabbat a holy day of rest

Sacred writings the holy books and other documents of a religious tradition

Segregation to separate people on the grounds of race or culture

Self-worth/self-esteem your own opinion of yourself

Service to work for a person or an organisation in order to help them

Sexuality the state of being straight, gay, lesbian, bisexual or transsexual

Spiritual dimension higher and purer consciousness beyond what is human, often linked to God

Symbolism the use of symbols to represent something

Tithing to pay a tenth of a person's income (usually to charity)

Tolerance to put up with, or even accept, other people's views and culture even if they are different to your own

Trade union a group of workers organised to help and protect workers in their own trade or industry

Ultimate questions a question for which there is no definite answer – e.g. life after death, creation – religion often provides answers to these

Unemployment to not have a paid job

United Nations (UN) a group of independent countries formed in 1945 to promote peace and security

Vocation a calling to work in a specific field; called by God for special work

Voluntary work a job/work done by choice, often without payment

Vows religious marriage promises

Work employment; physical or mental effort needed to do something

Index